FOR CHRISTOPHER M. HOGAN
1960 - 2018

This work would not have been realized without his inspiration, advice and knowledge of all things Queen Mary.

Dear Reader:

Those fascinated with the Art Deco beauty of the china, silver and crystal tableware commissioned by Cunard White Star especially for the *Queen Mary's* maiden voyage in 1936 have long faced a sad truth. Up until now a complete, well researched and comprehensive reference book did not exist.

So I began the task of building the catalog that I as a novice collector wished had been available to me. I spent years consulting leading *Queen Mary* authorities, museums and a managing director from Stuart Crystal. I tracked down elusive pattern book sketches and chuckled at tales from a couple of colorful former stewards. You now hold in your hands the reference book I hope will inform you in a handsome and entertaining format.

Wherever possible proper nomenclature is taken from period archival materials such as *Queen Mary* inventory listings, actual product catalogs and Stuart Crystal pattern books. Accurate measurements are provided throughout as well.

PHOTOGRAPHS BY JULIE M. HOGAN

The RMS *Queen Mary*'s China, Silver and Crystal

Designed and manufactured expressly for the RMS *Queen Mary*

By Julie M. Hogan

ON THE COVER:

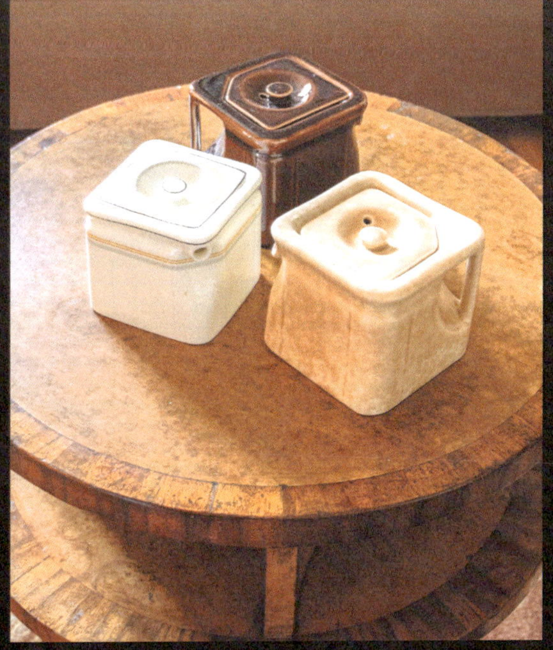

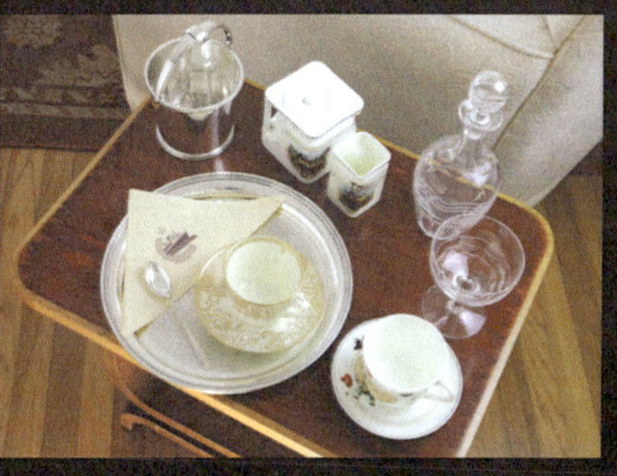

Painted cubeware, silver ice bucket, drinks tray, and crystal from RMS *Queen Mary*.

LEFT:

A variety of cubeware from *Queen Mary*.

BELOW:

En suite cup and saucer, Grosvenor cubeware, and crystal from the ship.

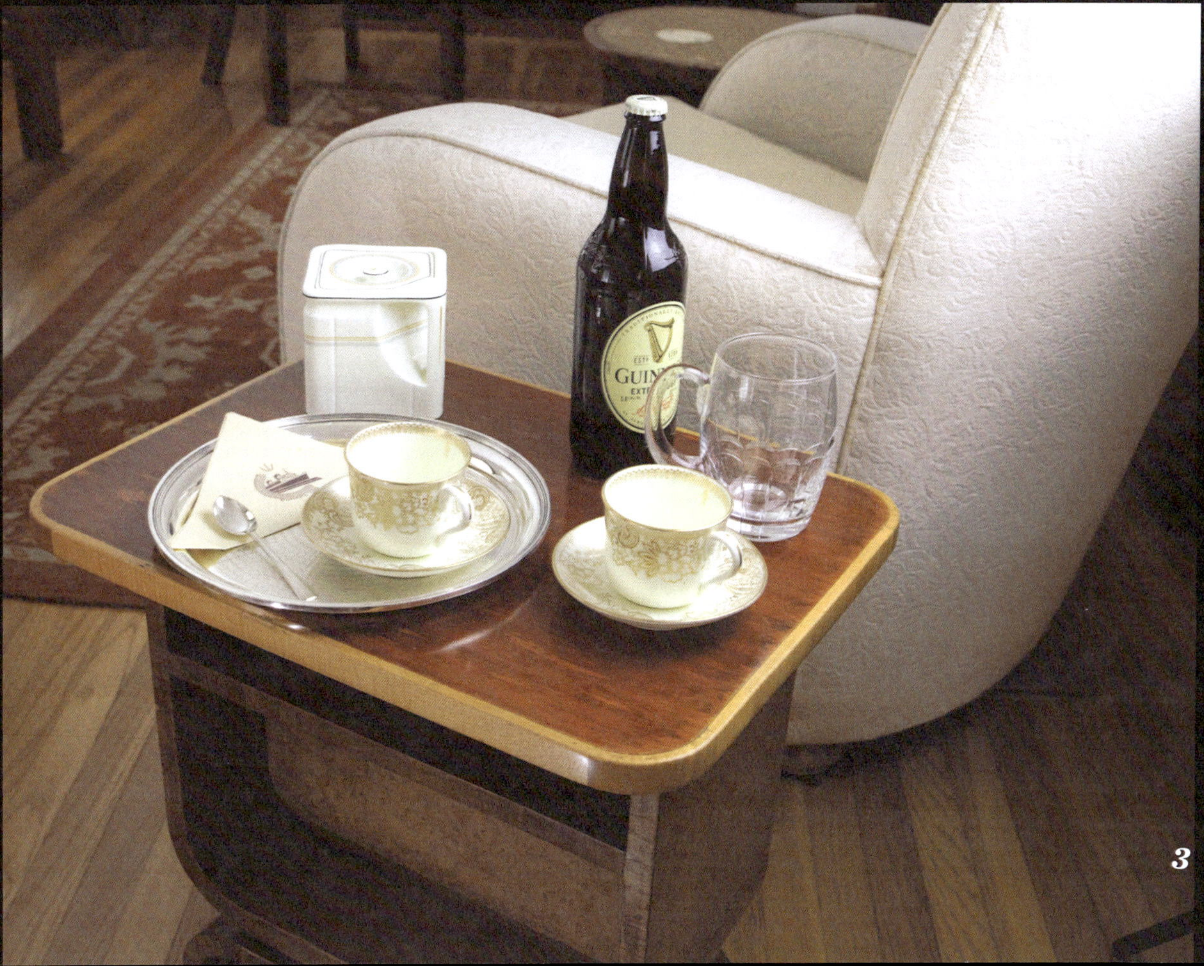

CONTENTS

5 The *Queen Mary*'s Crystal Table Glass

10 1936: Crest of the Wave

14 Postwar: Royal Brierly

16 1964: Cunard Pattern 'D' Georgian

26 Stuart Crystal Pattern Book Sketches for RMS *Queen Mary*

33 The *Queen Mary*'s China

36 En-Suite Service by Tuscan China Works

38 Grosvenor China Works / W.T. Copeland and Sons

40 E. Brain and Company / Foley China Works

46 John Maddock and Sons / 'Ivory Ware'

54 George Clews and Co., Ltd.

56 Ridgway / Booths Ltd.

57 Officers and Engineers Coffee Service

58 Copeland's Rose

60 Maker's Marks and Dates

65 The *Queen Mary*'s Silver Plate

68 Cake Stands and Fruit Stands

72 Wine Coolers and Ice Pails

76 Barware

78 Tableware

82 Silverware

84 Serveware

86 Miscellaneous

92 Elkington Maker's Marks and Date Codes

93 Elkington 1938 Hotel Plate catalog for RMS *Queen Mary*

The *Queen Mary's* Crystal Table Glass

This chapter is dedicated to all those who love
Stuart Crystal and the Queen Mary.

This section will document the wide range of crystal tableware patterns made for the Cunard Line from 1936 thru the late 1960s. There were several manufacturers and a range of shapes and sizes; you will find here as complete a representation as can be found anywhere. All of the crystal designed for *Queen Mary* was carried over to the *Queen Elizabeth* and later Cunard liners.

And, just as the Stuart catalogue notes: "As all these items are produced by hand, all measurements and capacities are approximate.'

PHOTOGRAPHS BY JULIE M. HOGAN

PREVIOUS PAGE:

A variety of crystal tableware from RMS *Queen Mary*.

Two crystal decanters from the ship.

Sherry Decanter and Glasses

DECANTER 8 1/2 INCHES HIGH / 21.5 CM
GLASSES 4 1/4 INCHES HIGH / 10.7 CM

This decanter and matching glasses were purchased directly from Stonier's department store in Liverpool. These were made by Stevens and Williams / Royal Brierley. There are two sizes to this decanter; shown is the smaller size.

'Excellent in shape, the ware conveys that sense of stability and durability one feels is essential for shipboard use.'
— *THE POTTERY GAZETTE AND GLASS TRADES REVIEW, 1946*

Spirit Decanter
11 INCHES HIGH / 28 CM

The decanter at right is from the estate of a purser who worked on board *Queen Mary*. As it is marked Cunard White Star, it is an early pattern from the 1930s. Many of the early pieces were decorated only with a star on the base.

1936: CREST OF THE WAVE

Deeply cut and faceted, this pattern is the oldest in the
Stuart Crystal pattern books for *Queen Mary*, dating to 1936.

Tankard Jug

7 INCHES HIGH / 17.75 CM
5 3/4 INCHES HIGH / 14.6 CM

Also called the Straight
Jug. This pattern is from
1936. There were at least
two sizes to this jug; the
one shown is the smaller.
The larger pitcher has one
more row of crescents.

Fruit Drink Jug

APPROX. 8 INCHES HIGH / 20.32 CM
6 1/2 INCHES HIGH / 16.5 CM

This shape is the same as the
Fruit Drink Jug for the similar
Carlingford pattern, although
this is a smaller (1 1/2 or
2 pt.) version than the one
pictured there. This also may
have served as a jug for ale.

The pitchers are called 'ice pitcher' or 'ice lipped' for the curvature of the spout which serves to keep ice inside when poured.

There are two sizes to the tankard glasses. See next page.

Shown here are some of the earliest and rarest crystal pieces designed for *Queen Mary*'s maiden voyage. Note their heavy polished bases, deeply cut swags and facet cuts.

Shown above is your Cunard White Star barware, an ever-present reminder of your favorite liner.

The souvenir whiskey tumblers have the Cunard belted logo etched on the base.

'... the "punty base" refers to the way tumblers were finished they did not have 'pontil' marks on the base they were still

Tankard Glass Pint
4 3/4 INCHES HIGH / 12 CM
16 OZ / 475 ML

Tankard Glass Half Pint
3 3/4 INCHES HIGH / 9.5 CM
8 OZ / 236 ML

A similar glass — *sans* handle — served as an ice tea glass. These beer mugs were designed for *Queen Mary* and made by Thomas Webbs and Sons Limited; shown are a pint and half-pint version.

on the base, even though the tumblers illustrated were blown in a mold and therefore ground and polished in the old style. This was quite costly but very pleasing to the eye.'

— ROGER PAULI

Soda Barrel Tumbler (¾ pt.)

4 1/2 INCHES HIGH / 11.5 CM
12 OZ / 355 ML

Barrel Tumbler (½ pt.)

3 3/4 INCHES HIGH / 9.5 CM
8 OZ / 236 ML

Barrel Tumbler (¼ pt.)

3 1/8 INCHES HIGH / 8 CM
4 OZ / 118 ML

Whiskey Tumbler

3 3/8 INCHES HIGH / 8.5 CM

Each of the barrel tumblers have 10 sets of swags and facet cuts as noted in the Stuart Crystal pattern book. This is the pattern first designed for *Queen Mary*: a photo of a similar glass is in *The Shipbuilder* from 1936.

To quote Roger Paulie: "These glasses were made with hand finished rims, the only item made this way post war until the late '50s. In 1968 there were still hundreds of them stored in wooden trays, awaiting use or destruction.'

POSTWAR: ROYAL BRIERLY

These glasses have a unique three line design, and form a distinct pattern of their own. There is a whole range of wine glasses as well as a pint glass in this pattern. Designed by Royal Brierly and Stevens and Williams, Ltd. for the *Queen Mary* and carried over later to the *Queen Elizabeth*.

Champagne Goblet

5 1/4 INCHES HIGH / 13.3 CM
9 OZ / 270 ML

Perhaps used for red wine, as seen in 1950s archivals; however, the Stuart Crystal pattern books name it as above.

The two glasses at left have rarely seen colored stems, and are shown alongside a tiny four line glass, perhaps for cordials or for absynth. This glass is a variant of the three line pattern, and is marked Webb Crystal.

Colored Stem

7 INCHES HIGH / 17.75 CM

Cordial

3 1/2 INCHES HIGH / 9 CM

Cocktail

4 3/8 INCHES HIGH / 11 CM
3 OZ / 80 ML

Known as the cordial but named Cocktail in the Stuart catalogues. This shape was also sold on board Cunard liners as souvenirs in the Stuart Crystal blue box; the foot of the glass was etched with your ship's name.

Liqueur

3 7/8 INCHES HIGH / 9.85 CM
2.5 OZ / 68 ML

1964: CUNARD PATTERN 'D' GEORGIAN

This pattern, etched with an undulating line above two rows of crescents, is dated to 1964 in the Stuart Crystal pattern book and titled Cunard Pattern 'D' Georgian.

The shapes shown here are not unique to the wave pattern. These same shapes carried the Stuart Crystal Beau, Carlingford, Elgin, Medley, Tamara, and Woodchester patterns. Carlingford was the biggest selling of these.

Cocktail

3 1/8 INCHES HIGH / 7.9 CM
3 OZ / 75 ML

Widely considered the small champagne glass, but properly named Cocktail and therefore used for a variety of mixed drinks.

'The founder of Stuart and Sons, Fred Stuart had commercial apprenticeship training before becoming a salesman. He was never a glassmaker by trade although he would have become knowledgeable over time. He is portrayed rather romantically as an orphan who started his apprenticeship at a very young age...but he was supported by his family, which included an uncle who was a London solicitor.'
— ROGER PAULI, FORMER MANAGING DIRECTOR, STUART CRYSTAL

Champagne (Low)

4 INCHES HIGH / 10.2 CM
6 OZ / 175 ML

Sometimes called the 'saucer' or 'flat' style champagne.

Champagne (Tall)

5 INCHES HIGH / 12.7 CM
6 OZ / 175 ML

Usually called a highball and double highball by collectors, these barrel tumblers were used more often for water.

Barrel Tumbler (½ pt.)

4 INCHES HIGH / 10 CM
8 OZ / 236 ML

Barrel (Soda) Tumbler (¾ pt.)

4 1/2 INCHES HIGH / 11.5 CM
12 OZ / 354 ML

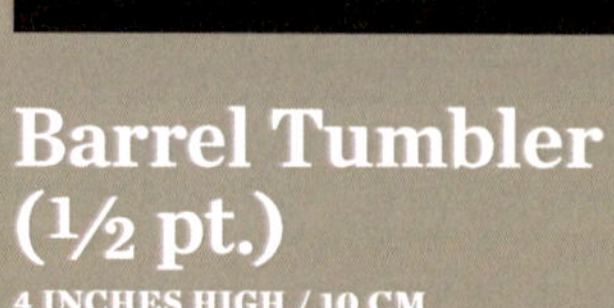

These are both postwar. It is interesting to note that when compared to the earlier pattern from 1936, the swags are now turned upside down. The 3/4 pint glass is also called a Soda Tumbler in the pattern book.

Old Fashioned Whiskey Tumbler

3 1/4 INCHES HIGH / 8.25 CM
6.5 OZ / 192 ML

This is the postwar cut for this tumbler.

A drinks menu from the *Queen Mary*.

'Matte intaglio. Plain foot. Punty base.'
— STUART CRYSTAL CUTTING INSTRUCTIONS (SOURCE: DR. ELEANOR FELDMAN)

The pattern stewards called 'Crest of the Wave' (left) is unnamed and unnumbered in the Stuart Crystal pattern books. Much later, in August 1964, the pattern at right is described and named Cunard Pattern 'D' Georgian.

— SOURCE: KEITH HALLETT, STEWARD, R.M.S. *MAURETANIA*

The nomenclature used here is taken from the Stuart catalog for the Cunard Pattern 'D' Georgian shapes.

Champagne Low/Tall	Claret	Sherry	Port	Cocktail	Tumbler (Straight)
The wide bowl of the coupe glass opens up the aromas and flavors—great for when you want to taste and experience the nuance of the sparkling wine, not just the effervescence of the bubbles. Use flutes when you're more focused on the bubbly aspect and less on the nuance of flavor.	Wider bowl for a full bodied wine. Most Claret (Bordeaux) blends have a bold, dry flavor. Its low sugar content relies more on the natural fruit taste.	A small bowl and narrow mouth help trap the complex aromas of the dry wine. A long stem stops hands from heating the drink.	Its very small size and narrow mouth reduces evaporation for this high alcohol wine.	A wide, shallow bowl for showcasing the drink's colors and allowing the aroma to develop.	A wide, robust base and plain design lets simple drinks speak for themselves. Made for filling with ice and a whisky of your choosing,

Above is a Stuart Crystal ice pail especially designed for the 'Olympic' class of ships that includes the *Titanic*. This one probably dates from the 1920s, an era prior to stabilizers being fitted to these huge ocean liners. A staggering amount of these must have ended up smashed and thrown overboard.

— ICE PAIL COURTESY OF JONATHAN QUAYLE, PURSER'S LOCKER

An advertisement for Whitbread's Superb Pale Ale in the 'luxurious comfort of the Cabin Lounge.'

THE ILLUSTRATED LONDON NEWS, SEPT. 26, 1936

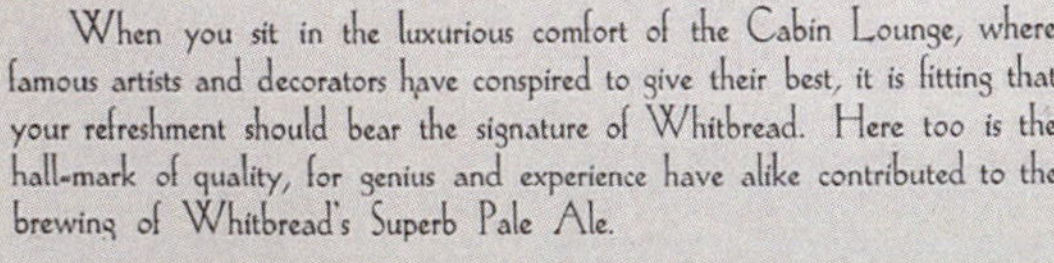

Plain, uncut glassware was perhaps reserved
for second and third class passengers, but it
is seen in first class archivals as well.

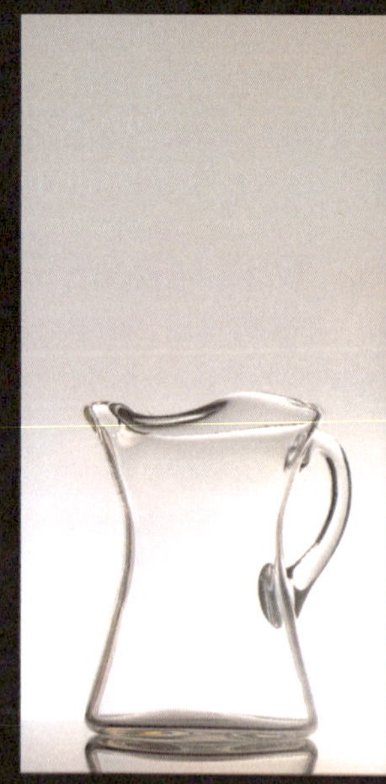

Ice Water Jug
(Large, Plain)
8 1/8 INCHES HIGH / 20.6 CM
48 OZ / 1419 ML

Ice Water Jug
(Small, Plain)
5 3/8 INCHES HIGH / 13.6 CM
20 OZ / 575 ML

Plain large and small jugs. First class pitchers
carry the customary rows of crescents.

Marking a pattern. The archivals on these two pages
are from a Stuart Crystal promotional catalog.

The smoother cutting a pattern.

CARLINGFORD
SERVICE NO.
27519

GOBLET · CHAMPAGNE (LOW) · CHAMPAGNE (TALL) · CLARET · SHERRY · PORT · LIQUEUR · COCKTAIL

PINDER BOWL · ICE PLATE · ICED TEA · ¾ PT. TUMBLER · ½ PT. TUMBLER · ⅜ PT. TUMBLER · ¼ PT. TUMBLER

SPIRIT DECANTER · QUART JUG · FRUIT JUICE · QUART E.D. JUG · QUART DECANTER

	CAPACITY ozs.	CAPACITY c/ltrt.	HEIGHT ins.	HEIGHT c/in
Sherry	2¾	8	4¼	10.5
Port	2¼	7	3⅞	9.2
Cocktail	3½	10	3⅞	8.5
Claret	4¼	13	4¼	10.8
„ L/S	5½	15	4⅞	14.7
Champagne	5¾	16.5	4¼	10.5
„ Tall	5¼	15.5	5	12.8
Liqueur	2	7.3	3¼	8.3
Goblet	9¼	76.5	4¾	12.6
„ S/S	6¼	18.25	4¾	11
Hock	6	14	6¾	17
Sherkes	5¼	13.5	3¼	8.3
Decanter, Liqueur	10	20.5	6¾	16.8
„ Wine	30	84	8¾	22.3
„ Claret (Hw)	30	84	10	25.2
Spirit Decanter, Round	27	77	8¾	22.2
„ „ Square	27	77	9¼	23.5
Tumbler, Barrel	7½	7	2⅞	6.18
„ „	5	14	3¼	8.4
„ „	8	21	3⅞	9.8

	CAPACITY ozs.	CAPACITY c/ltrs.	HEIGHT ins.
Tumbler, Barrel	10	28	4¼
„ „	15	42.5	4⅝
„ Straight	5	14	3⅞
„ „	7½	21	3⅞
„ „	10	28	4
„ „	13	37	5
Jug, 1 pt.	20	57	5¼
„ 1½ pt.	30	86	5⅞
„ 2 pt.	40	114	5¼
Old Fashioned Tumbler	7	20	3¼
„ „	10	28	3⅜
„ „	14	43	4¾
Iced Tea or Shandy	12½	34.5	6¼
Fruit Drink Glass	8	22.5	5¾
„ „	10	20.5	6¾
„ „	14	40	7¾
Fruit Drink Jug, 1½ qt.	20	86	8
„ „ 2 qt.	40	114	8⅝
„ „ 2½-qt.	60	173	9¼

As all these items are produced by hand, all measurements and capacities are approximate.

A page from a circa 1964 Stuart Crystal catalogue for the Carlingford pattern. It is intriquing to note that at the bottom of the page more shapes are listed; for example, there are three sizes for the fruit drink jug.

The Carlingford pattern. This pattern was produced between 1955 and 1968. Many of the same undecorated shapes— called blanks — were used for Cunard's Georgian pattern.

Four stages of glass cutting.

Following pages:
The Stuart Crystal
pattern book sketches
for RMS *Queen Mary*.

Right: The pattern first designed
for RMS *Queen Mary*; this first
page is labeled simply 'Cunard.'
Those pieces not decorated with
a wave had another nautical
element, a star, cut into the base.
These have a notation as to the
number of points. Each piece is
marked with the finished weight.

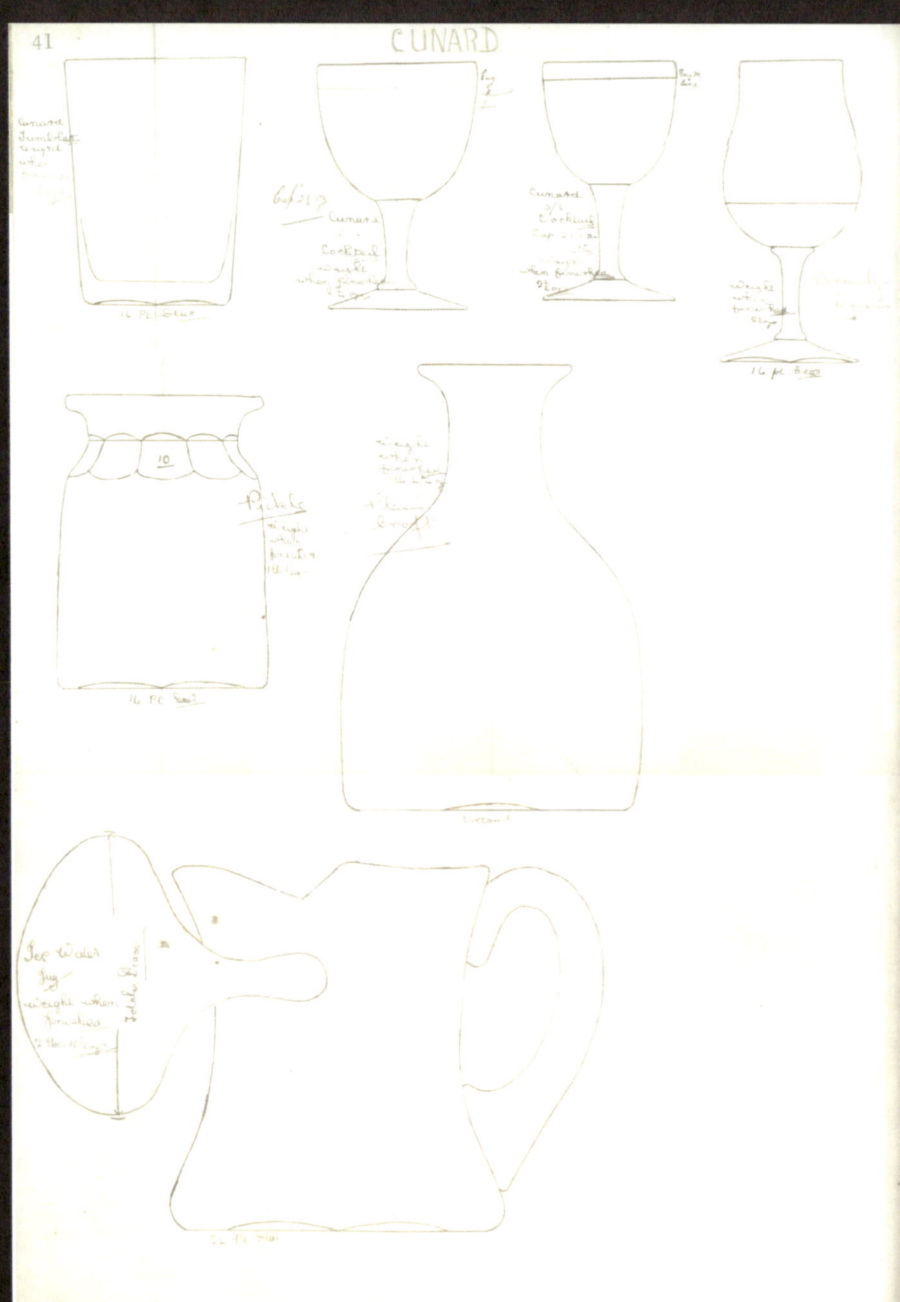

Left: This page is labeled 'Queen Mary' and dated January 1946. Larger tumblers are called soda tumblers. A notation is made next to the Whiskey Tumbler: 'Old Fashioned Whiskey Tumbler same without swags. Tourist Tumbler fluted only.' Designated pieces have the notation 'Tourist plain.'

Right: The tankard jug had at least two sizes.

Left: A stunning decanter.

Right: The page for the three-line pattern. Although this page is undated, *The Pottery Gazette* from 1946 shows photos of this pattern but lists Stevens and Williams Ltd. / Royal Brierly as designer and supplier for *Queen Mary*.

Left: The postwar 'Georgian' pattern. The crescents have reappeared but are upside down. Also, they are etched and not carved like the earliest pattern. Dated August 1964.

The *Queen Mary*'s China

CUBE Teapots Co., Ltd. of Leicester was formed in 1925 and ceased to trade in 1968.

Dear Reader:

Queen Mary's china service was carefully chosen to compliment the liner's striking interiors. Although the cube shape pre-dated WWI, the shape is unequivocally modern, and can be classed as an example of British Art Deco Modernism in its purest form. Fragile spouts and handles were done away with — the streamlined cube shape had been painstakingly perfected for stackability and to withstand the hardships of daily life onboard. In a subtle ivory tone to complement the liner's light wood paneling of native and exotic timbers, the gray and gold stripes were said to represent the sun's rays over the gray Atlantic. The china designed for *Queen Mary* was later put in use fleetwide and remained unchanged until 1968.

INTRODUCTION BY JONATHAN QUAYLE

PREVIOUS PAGE:

A Grosvenor tea set from RMS *Queen Mary*.

A variety of Cunard Grosvenor cubeware.

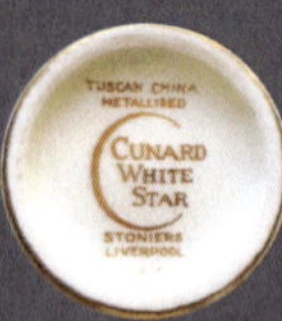

EN-SUITE SERVICE BY TUSCAN CHINA WORKS

This fragile tea service was reserved for VIPs and royalty in the suites, and was accorded the honor of having a conventional round teapot.

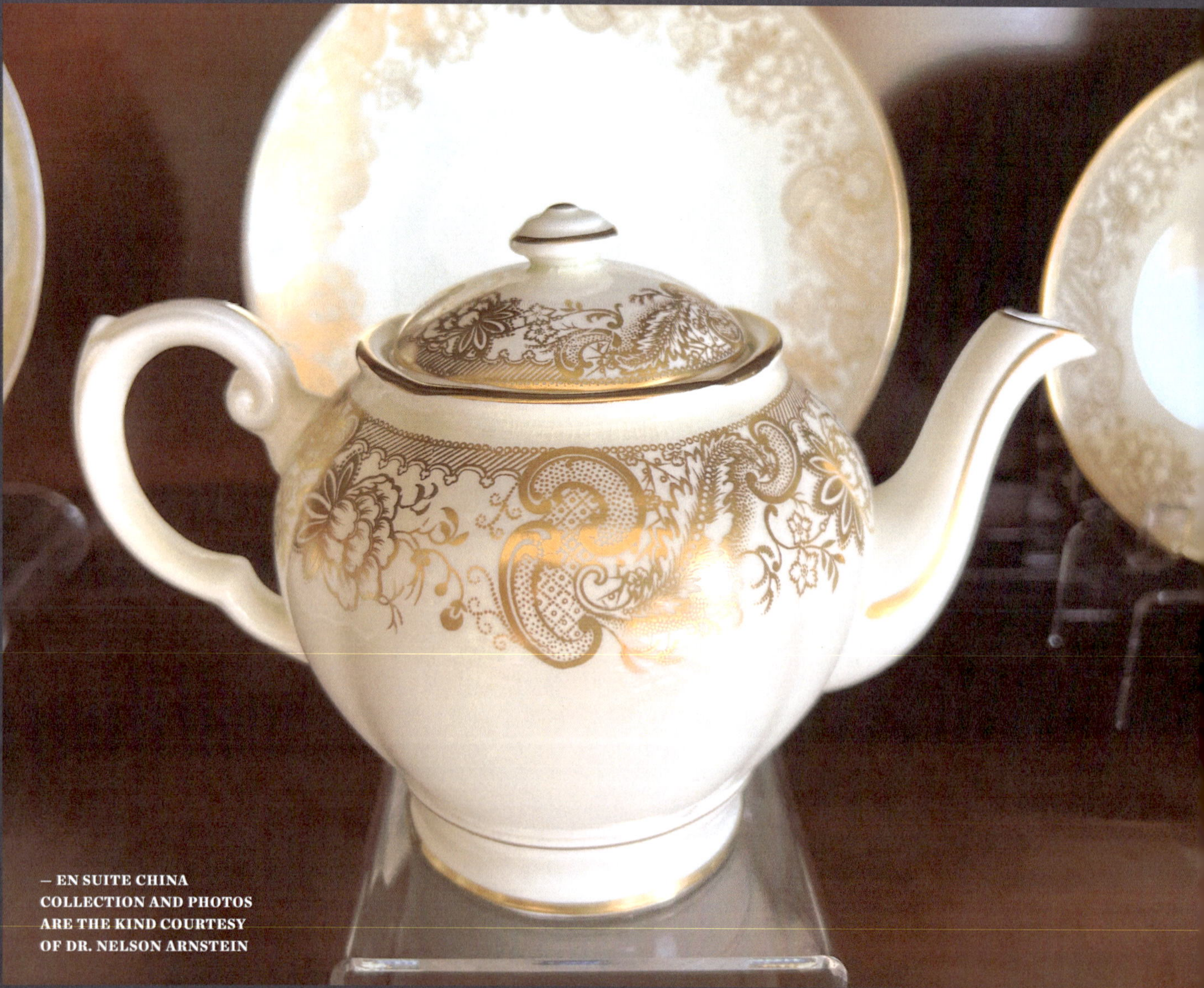

— EN SUITE CHINA COLLECTION AND PHOTOS ARE THE KIND COURTESY OF DR. NELSON ARNSTEIN

Teapot
5 INCH / 12.7 CM HIGH

Tea Plate
8 1/4 INCH / 21 CM DIAMETER

Bread and Butter Plate
6 1/2 INCH / 16.5 CM DIAMETER

Finished with real metallized gold. Specifically designed for use in the private suites on board *Queen Mary* in 1936 and later used on *Queen Elizabeth*. Very few pieces were produced, and these are only seen with the Cunard White Star mark. It is probable that this pattern had a 4-digit number and was never officially named; Tuscan had a large number of patterns and used a numbering system to make them easier to document and reorder.

Tools used for burnishing.

— SPODE MUSEUM

'Plant also supplied a tea service with a burnished gold print of "lace-like delicacy" in ivory china … it certainly suggests that the design would not have lasted long in normal service.'

— ANNE ANDERSON,
THE CUBE TEAPOT

Tea Cup and Saucer
CUP 3 1/8 INCH / 8 CM DIA.
SAUCER 5 1/8 INCH /
13 CM DIA.

Demi Cup and Saucer
SIZE NOT AVAILABLE /
NOT SHOWN

GROSVENOR CHINA WORKS / W.T. COPELAND AND SONS

Jackson & Gosling had been supplying these Grosvenor China tea sets to Cunard since 1936, but by 1949 E. Brain and Co. were supplying their Foley China as well. The Foley and Grosvenor sets were identical, with one difference: the early sets by Grosvenor were a richer, deeper shade of buff—this evolved over time to a lighter shade to offset the fading caused by the ship's dishwashers. This fine bone china was enjoyed by first class passengers, with a limited service in second class.

Copeland's Grosvenor China had been supplying Cunard since the early 1930s.

A comparison of Foley and Grosvenor tea cups.

Your steward dispensed a teaspoon of tea — most likely of the brand called Typhoo Tips — into the pot at the press of a button.

(Left) Few of the Grosvenor sets survive to this day. It appears they were produced for Cunard White Star from 1936-39, and for Cunard for a brief period from 1947 ending in the early 1950s. Those produced in 1936 are amongst the rarest and sport the same dark ivory tone as intended—this would gradually be replaced over time with a far paler production (shown above).

— JONATHAN QUAYLE

'[Foley] was "leaving no stone unturned" to bring out designs which were "thoroughly appreciative of the trend of modern furnishing." Foley's reputation was built on "simplicity of style and dignified plainness of shape"—their house style was very distinctive. After the war Foley supplied bone china CUBE shapes to the Queen Mary, *the* Queen Elizabeth *and the new* Mauretania, *in what became the standard Cunard pattern for bone china: bands of brown, grey and black.'*

— ANNE ANDERSON, *THE CUBE TEAPOT*

E. BRAIN AND COMPANY / FOLEY CHINA WORKS

By 1949, Foley bone china made by E. Brain and Company was supplementing the Grosvenor China tea sets.

Hot Water Jug (½ pint)

4 INCHES HIGH / 10 CM
2 1/2 INCHES SQUARE / 6.35 CM

Controversy rages over whether the milk be added before or after the hot water.

Teapot (½ pint)

3 1/4 INCHES HIGH / 8.25 CM
3 3/8 INCHES SQUARE / 8.5 CM

Teapot (1 pint)

3 3/4 INCHES HIGH / 9.5 CM
4 1/8 INCHES SQUARE / 10.5 CM

The small pot was used for a single passenger. The large was used for two or more passengers in the dining room.

Putting the milk in last was considered to be the 'correct' thing to do in refined social circles. Poor quality cups were inclined to crack when hot tea was poured into them, and putting the milk in first helped prevent this.

Cream Jug 2 oz.

2 7/8 INCHES HIGH / 7.3 CM
1 7/8 INCHES SQUARE / 4.75 CM

Sugar Basin 1 oz.

1 1/2 INCHES HIGH / 3.8 CM
2 INCHES SQUARE / 5 CM

For cubed sugar.

Slop Basin 4 oz.

1 3/4 INCHES HIGH / 4.44 CM
2 3/4 INCHES SQUARE / 7 CM

The waste tea leaves (slop) were placed within this cube.

Although square CUBE designs for cups, saucers, plates and even eggcups were available, Foley supplied Cunard with traditional round shapes for these.

Tea Cup and Saucer

CUP 3 INCHES DIAMETER / 7.62 CM
SAUCER 5 INCHES DIAMETER / 12.7 CM

Etiquette dictated stirring your tea back and forth, and not in a circular motion. The spoon must never bash the sides of the cup.

Demi Cup and Saucer

CUP 2 1/4 INCHES DIAMETER / 5.7 CM
SAUCER 4 3/8 INCHES DIAMETER / 11 CM

Used for Turkish coffee or espresso. Etiquette called for holding your cup by the handle without poking your finger through, and lifting the saucer from the table was a major *faux pas*.

Coffee Cup and Saucer

CUP 3 1/2 INCHES DIAMETER / 8.9 CM
SAUCER 5 3/4 INCHES DIAMETER / 14.6 CM

The rarity of these cups and saucers is telling.

Since the large tea plate would not fit on a bakelite tray, service was only in the Main Lounge and not on deck—hence the rarity of these plates.

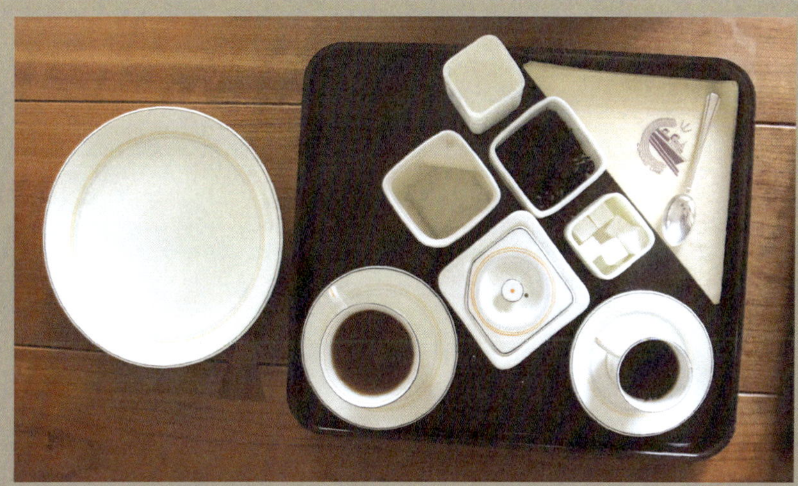

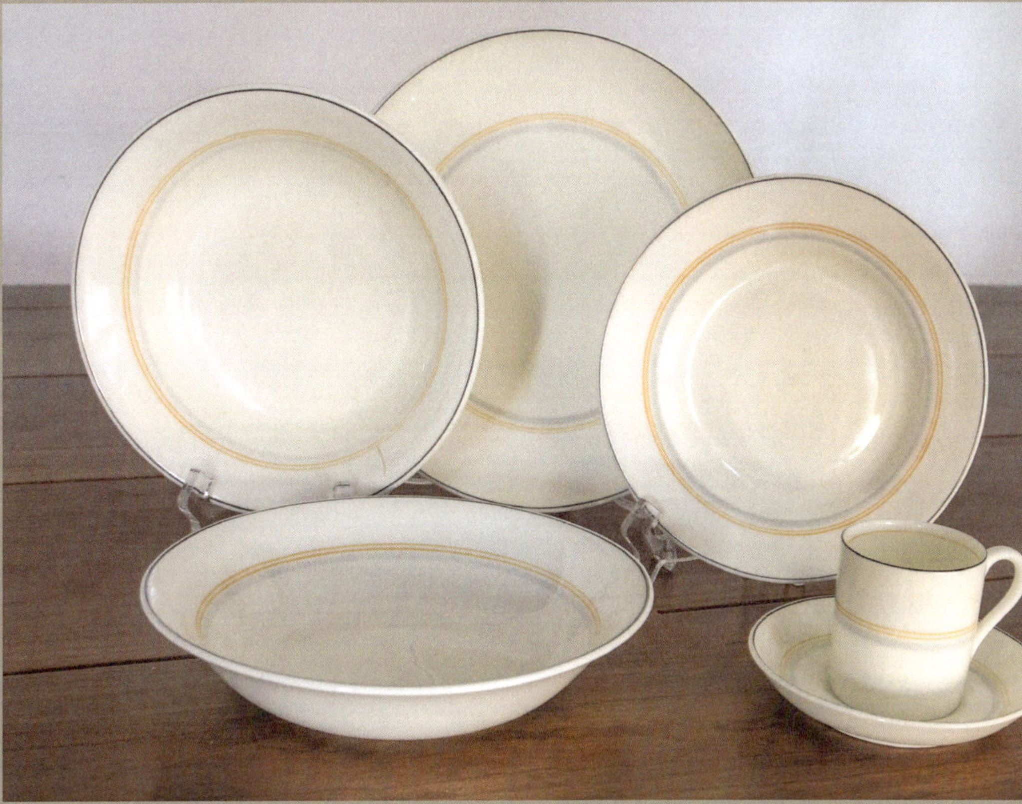

Cereal Bowl (left)

7 1/4 INCHES / 18.4 CM

Tea Plate (center)

8 1/2 INCHES / 21.6 CM

Bread and Butter Plate (right)

6 5/8 INCHES / 16.8 CM

Foley bone china provided for the passenger looking to enjoy a sweet treat as well.

Footed Sugar Basin

3 1/4 INCHES DIAMETER / 8.25 CM

Also called 'ice coupe.' Ice cream was referred to as 'ices,' hence the name; but it is referenced as above in the inventory listings.

Sweet Dish (Lobed)

6 INCHES DIAMETER / 15.25 CM
7 1/8 INCHES DIAMETER / 18.5 CM
9 1/2 INCHES DIAMETER / 24 CM

There are three sizes of the lobed bowls, the largest almost 9 1/2 inches across.

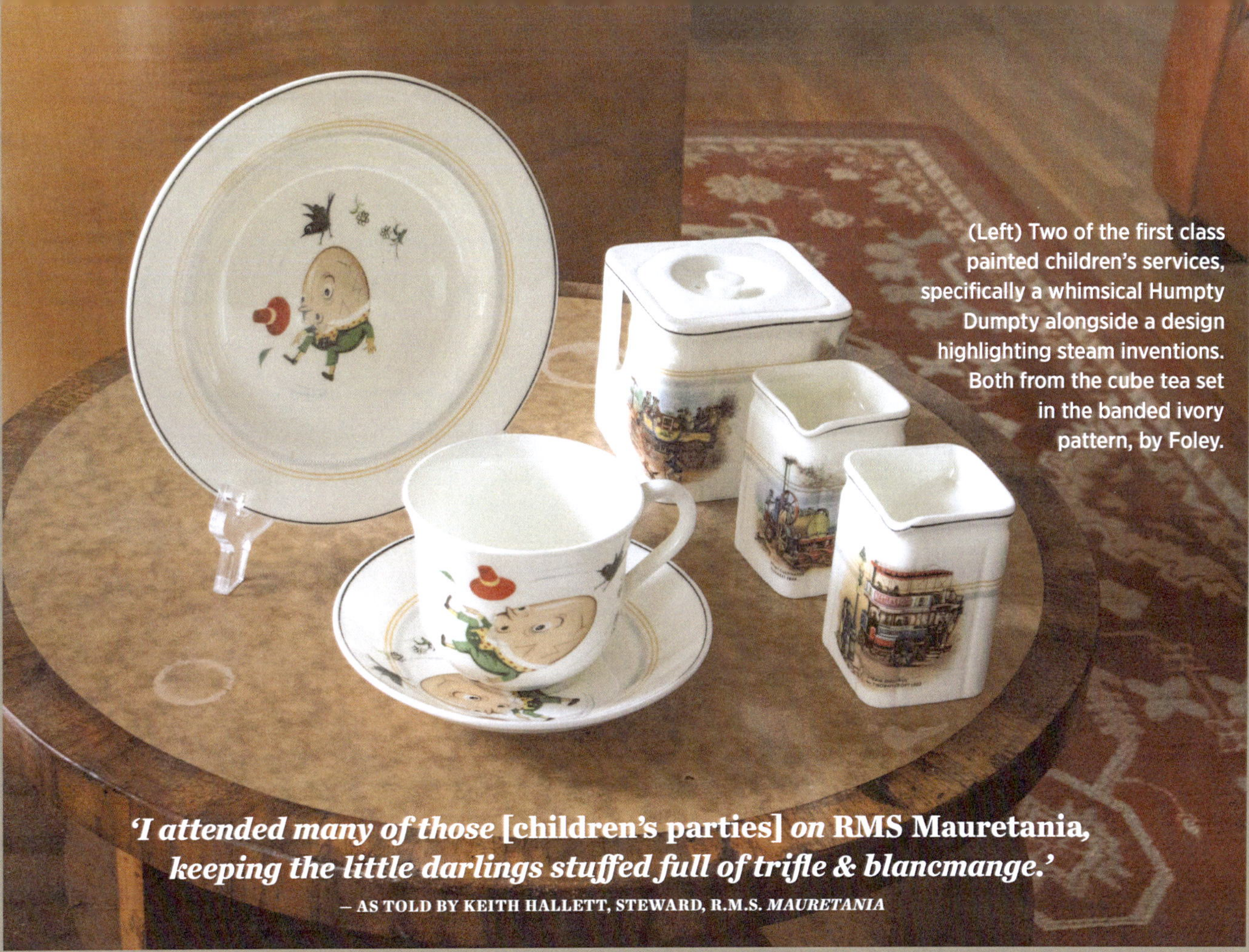

(Left) Two of the first class painted children's services, specifically a whimsical Humpty Dumpty alongside a design highlighting steam inventions. Both from the cube tea set in the banded ivory pattern, by Foley.

'I attended many of those* [children's parties] *on* RMS Mauretania, *keeping the little darlings stuffed full of trifle & blancmange.'

– AS TOLD BY KEITH HALLETT, STEWARD, R.M.S. *MAURETANIA*

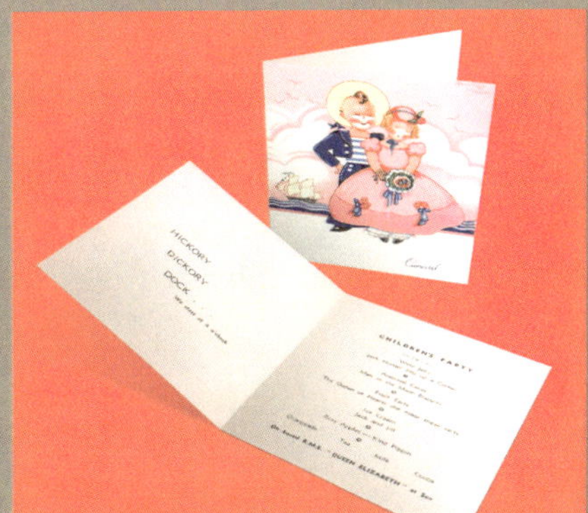

A Cunard children's party menu from *Queen Elizabeth*.

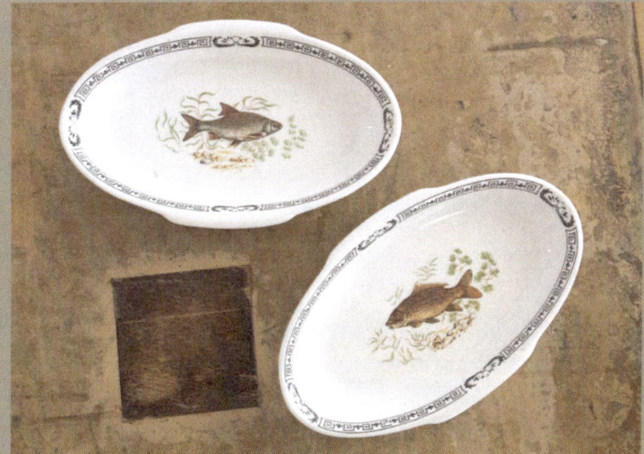

(Right) Painted china, probably for fish course, as used within the third class of the *Queen Mary*. In the black fruits pattern first designed for use on *Aquitania*.

John Maddock and Sons was a firm that catered specially for ship and hotel requirements and supplied earthenware to the new *Queen Mary* as well as other Cunard ships up until the late '60s.

JOHN MADDOCK AND SONS / 'IVORY WARE'

Maddock 'Ivory Ware' earthenware comprised the bulk of the service for first- and second-class passengers, a handsome and sturdy design that closely matched the finer Foley banded bone china.

Salad Bowls

6 3/4 INCHES DIAMETER / 17 CM
8 1/4 INCHES DIAMETER / 21 CM
11 1/2 INCHES DIAMETER / 29.3 CM

There are three sizes of these large bowls.
Pictured at right and below are the two smaller sizes.

Eggcup

2 INCHES DIAMETER / 5 CM

Used for your morning
boiled egg.

Breakfast Cup

CUP 3 3/4 INCHES DIAMETER / 9.525 CM
SAUCER 6 1/8 INCHES DIAMETER / 15.55 CM

For coffee. Used for
breakfast in first class.

Consommé Cup

CUP 3 3/4 INCHES DIAMETER / 9.525 CM
SAUCER 6 1/8 INCHES DIAMETER / 15.55 CM

Two-handled cup for bullion (beef
tea). Used for breakfast in first class.

Soup Plate

9 INCHES DIAMETER / 23 CM

Crescent Salad Plate

8 INCHES BY 4 3/4 INCHES / 20 CM BY 12 CM

Used as a side plate for salad, nesting neatly beside your dinner plate.

Dinner Plate

9 5/8 INCHES DIAMETER / 24.5 CM

Pudding Plate

6 1/8 INCHES DIAMETER / 15.8 CM

Celery Plate

8 1/4 INCHES BY 4 3/4 INCHES / 21 CM BY 12 CM

Cheese Plate

7 1/4 INCHES DIAMETER / 18.5 CM

Flat Salad Plate

8 1/8 INCHES DIAMETER / 20.5 CM

Cereal Plate

7 1/2 INCHES DIAMETER / 19 CM

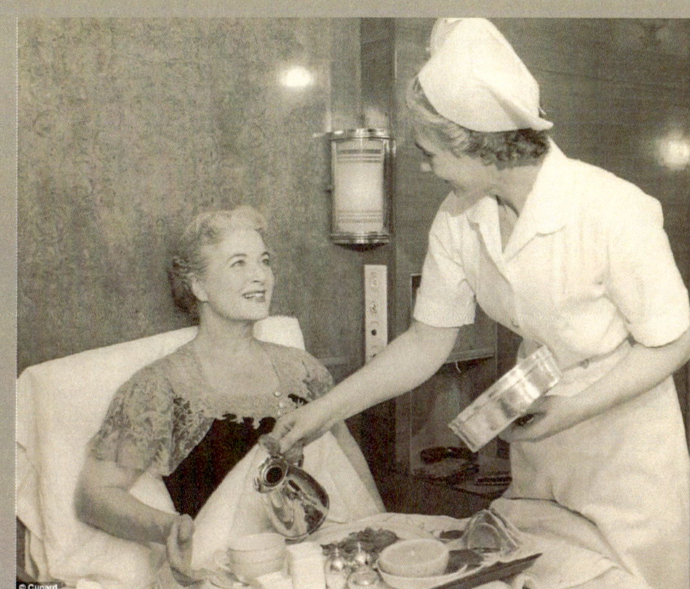

'Dinner and breakfast crockery for the cabin and tourist classes have been supplied by Messrs. John Maddock & Sons, Ltd., of Burslem. The ware comprises plates for meat, soup, salad, sweets and cheese, as well as hors d'oeuvre dishes, salad bowls, breakfast cups and saucers, consommé cups and stands, and egg-cups, representing an aggregate of about 30,000 pieces.'

— THE SHIPBUILDER AND MARINE ENGINE-BUILDER, JUNE 1936

The nomenclature at left is per the Cunard inventory listings.

Maddock 'Ivory Ware' came in a wide array of shapes and sizes, designed to serve passengers quickly and easily.

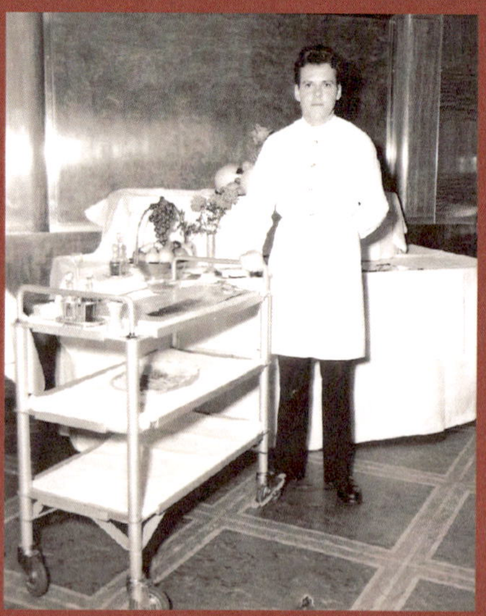

Hors d'oeuvre Dish (Nos. 1 thru 3)

5 7/8 BY 6 3/4 INCHES / 15 CM BY 17.125 CM

Hors d'oeuvre Dish Wagon (No. 4)

5 1/2 INCHES BY 8 7/8 INCHES / 14 CM BY 22.5

The (No. 4) rectangle trays, once filled with *hors d'oeuvres*, were placed on a rotating trolley and wheeled to your tableside — a quick and efficient way to offer passengers their choice of *aperitif*. There are two sizes of the rectangle trays. The rounded dishes have left- and right-handed shapes, these were placed in a group of four—perfect to serve four people at a table.

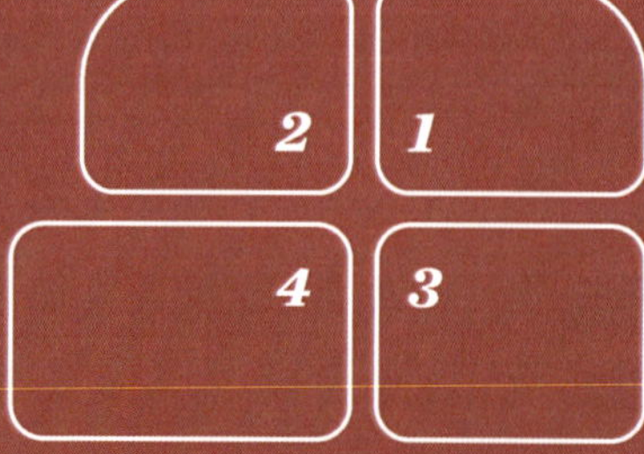

Each shape is numbered on the back.

50

A circa 1950s Cunard advertisement showing some of the 'gustatory delights' awaiting its passengers.

A steward taking stock of new china in one of *Queen Mary*'s private dining rooms. Older stewards were in charge of crockery and silverware — they were 'Crockery Kings' or 'Silver Kings.' It's assumed that they had to account to the Chief Steward for any shortages.

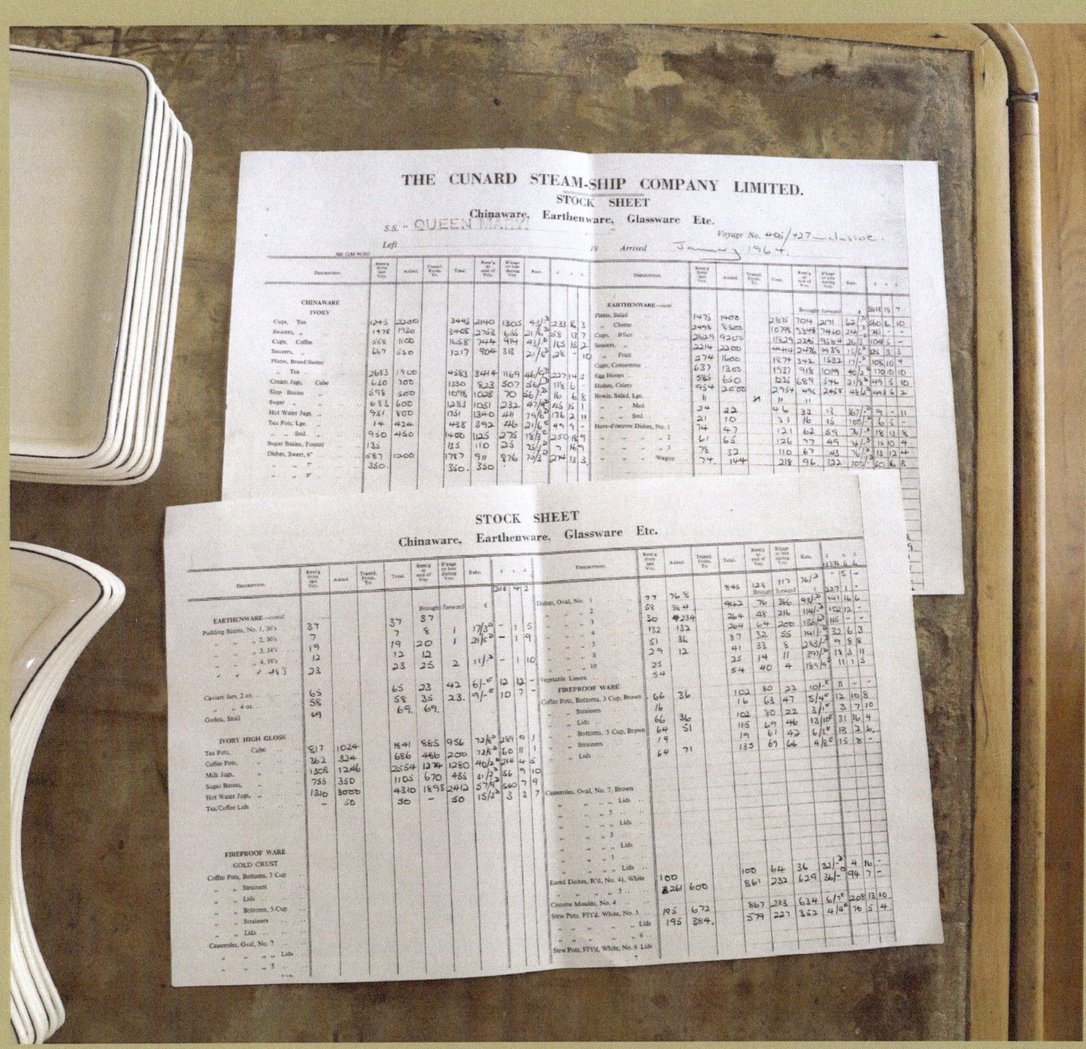

Inventory sheets for Cunard *Queen Mary*'s 405th thru 427th voyages, showing orders, rates and breakages for Foley china and Maddock earthenware. As an example, 9,584 Maddock breakfast cups were recorded as 'Breakage or Loss' during those voyages.

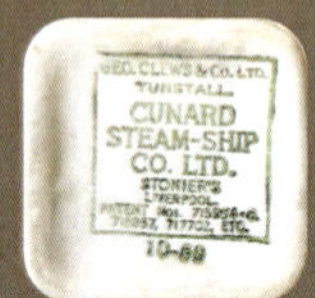

By the '50s Clews was making a white glazed breakfast set. This was then replaced by identical pieces made by Sadler when they became a Cunard supplier.

GEORGE CLEWS AND CO., LTD.

George Clews of Tunstall supplied stoneware breakfast sets in this matte oatmeal glaze, used for morning tea and breakfasts served in the staterooms, as well as on deck for third class.

(Clockwise from top left)

Cream Jug
3 INCHES HIGH / 5 CM
2 INCHES SQUARE / 5 CM

Slop
1 7/8 INCHES HIGH / 4.75 CM
2 3/8 INCHES SQUARE / 6.5 CM

Coffee Pot
4 5/8 INCHES HIGH / 11.75 CM
2 3/4 INCHES SQUARE / 7 CM

Hot Water Jug
4 1/2 INCHES HIGH / 11.5 CM
2 3/8 INCHES SQUARE / 6.5 CM

Tea Pot
3 1/4 INCHES HIGH / 8.25 CM
3 3/8 INCHES SQUARE / 9.25 CM

Sugar
1 1/2 INCHES HIGH / 40 MM
2 INCHES SQUARE / 50 MM

'... plain CUBE pieces were used for serving breakfast and tea in the cabins, alongside a metal thermos jug and banded earthenware pieces of the type supplied by Maddock & Son.'

— ANNE ANDERSON, *THE CUBE TEAPOT*

'Perhaps a typical example of how articles of everyday utility are now being made in pleasing, as well as functional, form without loss of that simplicity which is characteristic of all really good design.'
— THE POTTERY GAZETTE AND GLASS TRADES REVIEW, MARCH 1936

Ridgway Pottery later merged with the Booths & Colclough China Company during the 1940s, and became a part of Royal Doulton in 1972.

RIDGWAY / BOOTHS LTD.

Third class on *Queen Mary* enjoyed the gold fruits pattern that was old stock from first class on *Mauretania/ Aquitania/Berengaria*. As that supply was exhausted, the black fruit pattern took the dominant service in third from the 1950s to 1967.

(Left) The golden pattern originally chosen for use on *Mauretania* is sometimes referred to as the Mauretania pattern. Later used fleet wide on the ship's sister ships, *Aquitania* and *Berengaria*. There is also a simpler gold pattern with a thin gold band.

An example of each of the three patterns is shown below.

OFFICERS AND ENGINEERS

This plain white china was exclusively used for the officers in the wardroom and other officer and senior ratings spaces.

(Below) A delicate fine bone china coffee cup by MInton with the black rampant lion logo from the early 1900s. As far as it is known, this pattern was used in the third class of earlier liners, and then used onboard the *Lusitania* and *Mauretania* in the Verandah Palm Courts. The latest this piece was used was onboard the *Queen Mary* before the war.

Minton Coffee Cup

CUP 2 1/4 INCHES DIA. / 5.75 CM
SAUCER 4 5/8 INCHES DIA. / 11.75 CM

At right is the earlier coffee cup by Minton. The plain white version is shown at right in the photo below.

Scalloped Shells

3 3/8 INCHES / 8.5 CM
4 3/4 INCHES / 12 CM

(Above) There are two sizes of these escalloped shell dishes by Minton; they were used when sliced lemon was desired with your tea. The larger shell was used for more than one passenger. These were designed for *Queen Mary* in 1936 and later produced by Foley as well.

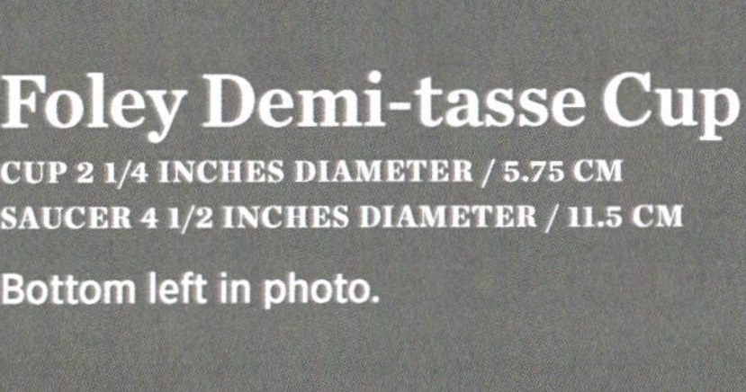

Wedgwood Demi-tasse Cup

CUP 2 1/4 INCHES DIAMETER / 5.75 CM
SAUCER 4 1/2 INCHES DIAMETER / 11.5 CM

Top left in photo.

Foley Demi-tasse Cup

CUP 2 1/4 INCHES DIAMETER / 5.75 CM
SAUCER 4 1/2 INCHES DIAMETER / 11.5 CM

Bottom left in photo.

First used onboard liners like the *Aquitania* during the '20s and '30s, Grosvenor's Rose pattern was carried over and used onboard *Queen Mary* from 1936 up to the 1950s, within second class. The earliest pieces carry the Cunard belted logo. By the 1950s this same pattern was being produced by Foley, making it a pattern with a very long production run for Cunard indeed. An entire tea service was produced.

Cubeware and chinoiserie both enjoyed great popularity in the 1920s, when Cunard liners carried the Cuckoo, Bird of Paradise and Currants patterns. Below left: Minton's Cuckoo on its tray. Below right: A variety of Cunard chinoiserie cubeware.

After the Cunard/White Star mergers, the other Cunard liners retained their existing china patterns. Bird of Paradise and all its variants, so easily confused, emerged around 1915 with the advent of *Aquitania*; these carry the original Cunard mark. They remained in use on *Aquitania* and *Mauretania* until the early 1930s. With the Depression, Cunard would have used up old stocks; no marks are seen dating these later than the late 1920s.

These patterns are so similar — especially on the smaller shapes — to identify them it may be easiest to instead simply turn the piece over to reveal its manufacturer's mark.

(Left) Plant's Tuscan China 'Bird of Paradise' was supplied to *Lusitania*, *Mauretania* and *Aquitania*, notably for Souvenir ware.

(Center) Minton supplied their 'Cuckoo' pattern in bone china, this pattern first appearing in the early 1800s.

(Right) Copeland's Spode supplied 'Currants' cubeware, the pattern first appearing around 1825 and later introduced to Cunard in 1912.

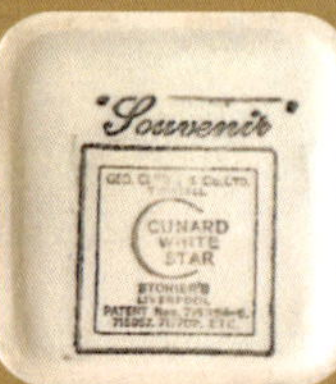

MAKER'S MARKS AND SOUVENIRS

Cunard's fine china was, not surprisingly, coveted by passengers as a momento of their crossing. Well aware of this, Cunard had long cut their lossses and satisfied this desire by ordering items matching their in-service china marked 'souvenir' and made available for purchase on board.

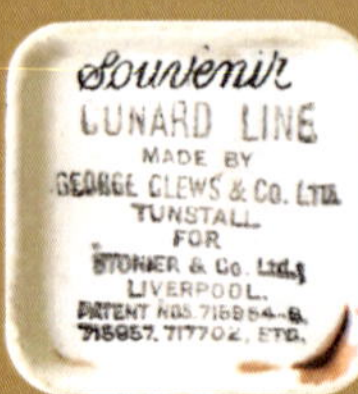

The Clews earthenware tea sets were available as souvenirs, in both oatmeal and this dark brown glaze.

The Clews oatmeal earthenware was available as a souvenir. Clews pieces after 1949 are found with a white glaze identical to the Sadler.

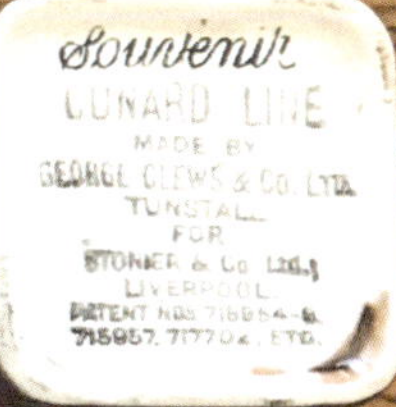

Alongside the in-service Grosvenor and Foley tea sets designed for *Queen Mary*, Cunard White Star commissioned the same richly toned sets as souvenirs.

While Tuscan's Bird of Paradise was available as a souvenir, the Copeland's Rose pieces were not.

The group of dots and/or dashes on the bottom of your china are not accidental. The painter decorating the piece would 'sign' his handiwork, as he was paid on piece rates. The decorated china shown on these pages was typically a combination of hand painting and transferware, where ink was transferred via a paper stencil that was rubbed on to the body. At right: Applying a stencil at the Minton factory.

'*There was a specific way that Cunard would lay a table…it had to be perfect. I've seen a head waiter go to a table, and if he wasn't satisfied with it, all he needed to do was get a corner of the table cloth and just pull it slightly to one side. And the whole thing would have to be done again.*'

— *ADVENTURES ON THE* QUEEN MARY…*TALES OF A TEENAGE CREW MEMBER*
BY DAVE WOODERS WITH JAMES RADFORD

A recreated table setting from *Queen Mary*. Table settings were inspected by the headwaiter to ensure that the legendary Cunard level of perfection was met.

An early
photo of
tables set
for service
in the first
class dining
room, looking
forward.

The *Queen Mary*'s Silver Plate

Dear Reader:

To cater for *Queen Mary*'s First Class passengers, Cunard White Star employed the best silversmith of the day, Elkington Plate, pioneers in the field of silver plating metal since the 1850s.

They were commissioned by Cunard White Star to produce a service that would be striking yet capture the spirit of the age, and compliment the interiors of the Cunarder. The pattern became known as 'Plain Pine' or 'Pinewood,' a nod to the ship's wood panelled interiors. The service was a beautiful balance of what would later become known as British Art Deco and modernism, and it represents one of the purest forms of modernism found onboard a ship at the time. The result was a comfortable 'homely' feel, like the well-loved interior of a great country estate.

INTRODUCTION BY JONATHAN QUAYLE

A silver fruit stand from
RMS *Queen Mary*.

Kettle with Stand
13 1/4 INCHES HIGH / 33.6 CM

Ebonized handle. The kettle is pinned to the stand using two chains, and the burner removes for refilling with fuel. Used to replenish teapots when serving tea in the private dining rooms.

'In those days only two meals were served each day, a large breakfast and a large dinner in the evening. The idea of having tea, sandwiches and cakes in the afternoon, to tide them over until Dinner time, became very popular.'
— AS TOLD BY KEITH HALLETT, STEWARD, R.M.S. MAURETANIA

Tea time on board RMS *Caronia* in the fifties.

3-Tiered Cake Stand

STAND 19 INCHES HIGH / 48.25 CM
TRAYS 8 1/4 INCHES DIAMETER / 21 CM

Passengers relaxing on deck were brought a selection of sandwiches and tempting nibbles on this three-tiered stand at afternoon tea time.

Besides sandwiches, the stand might hold small assorted cakes, usually square, that the stewards called Tab-Nabs. The top tray would probably contain traditional scones, to be spread with clotted cream and strawberry jam.

Associated trays are specifically designed to fit snugly into their tiers and are distinct from the round chargers.

The fruit stands, although identical in shape, were made in two finishes: silver plate was used in the suites while the first class dining room used solid bronze with a gold finish. These were also supplied without the handle.

Fruit Stand (Silver)

**14 INCHES / 10.25 CM HIGH
(INCLUDING HANDLE)**

Shown with the silver plate finish. Grapes hung suspended from the handle.

Fruit Stand (Bronze)

**14 INCHES / 10.25 CM HIGH
(INCLUDING HANDLE)**

The finish is real gold with a lacquer coating. These baskets were one of the few items on the ship to have a hand-hammered finish.

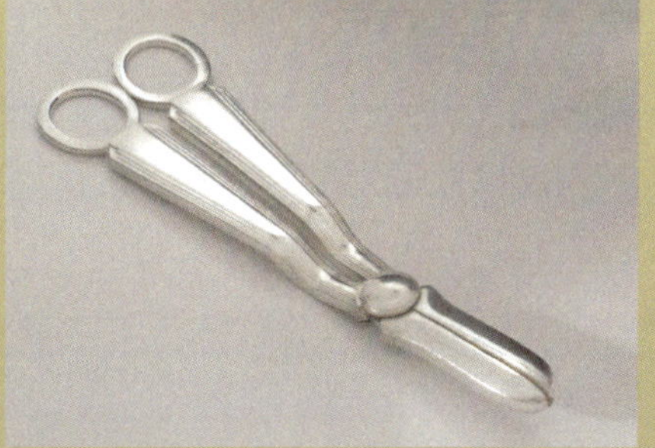

Grape scissors, used for snipping individual grapes off their stems.

This elegant vase displayed the fresh flowers kept onboard. Although commonly referred to as Art Deco, *Queen Mary* is thoroughly Streamline Moderne.

A fruit basket was a traditional gift to those embarking on a crossing, harking back to the days when scurvy was the scourge of ocean travel.

A variety of coolers were used on board. From champagne to caviar, these were used to keep the finer things in life chilled.

This pierced drainer for the wine cooler at near right kept the bottle dry above the melting ice.

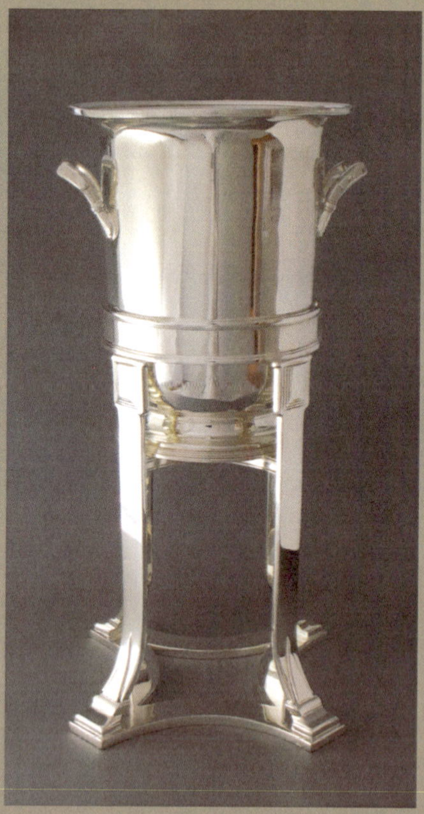

Wine Cooler

**6 1/4 INCHES / 15.875 CM HIGH
(INCLUDING HANDLE)**

Used to cool 'splits' or demi champagne bottles.

Wine Cooler with Stand

**COOLER 9 5/8 INCHES / 24.5 CM HIGH
ONE QUART / .94 LITER**

STAND 12 5/8 INCHES / 32 CM HIGH

The wine steward had the job of bringing the champagne and cooler to your dining room table as required.

The unique combination of wine cooler and stand allowed these to be placed on the deck beside your dining room table—thus saving valuable table space while keeping your chilled champagne bottle conveniently within arm's reach of your waiter.

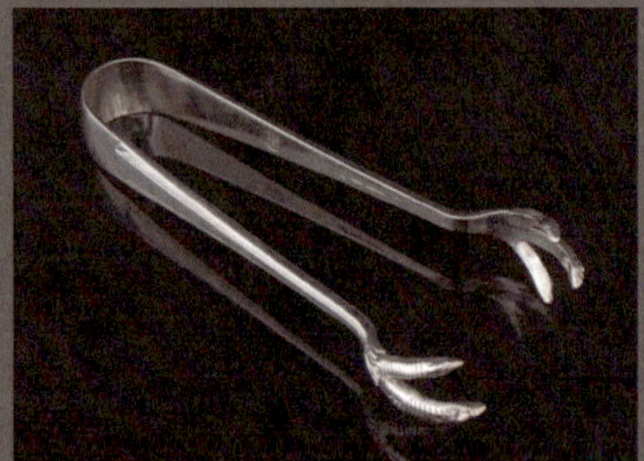

These talon-like tongs were used for serving ice cubes.

Ice Pail

PAIL 5 5/8 INCHES / 14.25 CM HIGH
(INCLUDING HANDLE)
TRAY 6 1/4 INCHES DIAMETER

Shown with its associated drip tray. It may also have been fitted with a drainer.

Caviar Cooler

6 7/8 INCHES / 17.5 CM HIGH
(INCLUDING HANDLE)

This came with a glass insert to hold the caviar above the ice. This pail carries the Cunard Steamship mark and is hallmarked Walker and Hall, dating to 1929; however the similarities to the later Plain Pine pattern are striking.

'The Bon Voyage parties were quite busy affairs… It was only a short time guests were allowed on board on Sailing Day, so quite a frantic time for stewards to satisfy demand for cubed ice. They brought their own champagne and booze. Stewards provided the ice and glassware (a good source of tips). All your friends took a taxi down to the ship….What Fun! Brilliant, then that voice came over the speakers. "All visitors ashore please," then we Stewards had to clean up.'
– AS TOLD BY KEITH HALLETT, STEWARD, R.M.S. MAURETANIA

A wine steward's badge from the *Queen Mary*, in the Plain Pine pattern chosen especially for the ship.

— COURTESY OF JONATHAN QUAYLE, PURSER'S LOCKER

'Strength all depends upon shape, thin there, thicker there, light at the top, heavy at bottom or as the case may be.'

— *THE STUDIO* MAGAZINE, MARCH 1936

Alcoholic beverages have always been the highlight of a crossing; these items take serving to a high art.

Cocktail Shaker

10 1/4 INCHES / 26 CM HIGH

Cocktail Shaker

8 1/8 INCHES / 20.6 CM HIGH

The smaller shaker is marked Cunard White Star. While the larger shaker carries the White Star Line markings, quite often after the merger White Star Line items were brought over to the Cunard White Star ships.

Round Waiter Tray (10 ⅜")

10 3/8 INCHES / 27 CM DIAMETER
12 3/8 INCHES / 32 CM DIAMETER
17 INCHES / 43 CM DIAMETER

Inscribed with an engine turned (machine engraved) fine geometric pattern. Dazzling. There are several sizes of the drink trays, the largest being 17 inches across; shown is the 10 inch size.

Wine Strainer

6 1/4 INCHES / 15.8 CM HIGH

Funnel with separate strainer. Used to aerate wine while decanting.

Escargot Tray and Tongs

TRAY 5 3/4 INCHES / 14.6 CM DIAMETER   TONGS 6 INCHES / 15.25 CM LONG

The tongs were provided to hold the shell while a slender two-pronged fork (not shown) would be used to remove the meat. The tray and tongs are not marked, but they are from *Queen Mary*.

This elegant tableware graced tables on board.

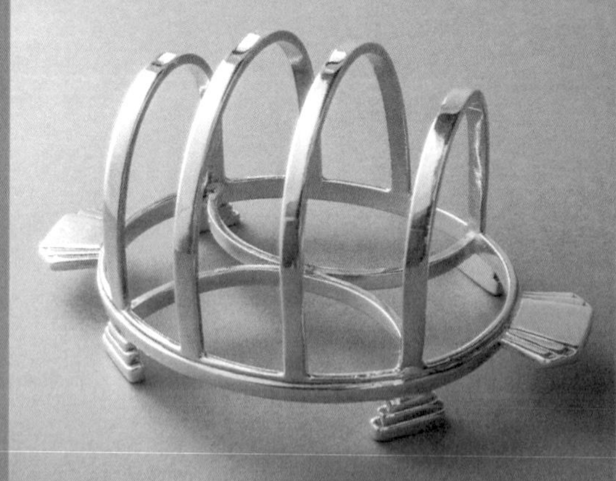

Sauce Boat (Large)

8 1/4 INCHES / 21 CM LONG
(INCLUDING HANDLE)

On a pedestal foot. For cream, sauce or gravy.

Sauce Boat (Small)

6 1/8 INCHES / 15.5 CM LONG
(INCLUDING HANDLE)

Toast Rack

5 3/4 INCHES/ 14.6 CM LONG
(INCLUDING HANDLES)

This rack held toast sliced into triangles and allowed them to cool; they were then spread with chilled butter—a preference more British than American.

Finger Bowl

4 1/8 INCHES / 10.5 CM DIAMETER

This bronze bowl was filled with slightly warmed water and a thin slice of lemon or a few flower petals, and used to rinse your fingers before your desert course. *The Studio* Magazine observed that the hand-hammered finish 'seems to be rather out of place among so many other machine-made articles of plain design.' Made to match the bronze fruit basket.

— KIND COURTESY OF TIMOTHY GARLINGHOUSE

Butter Dish and Drainer

5 INCHES / 12.75 CM DIAMETER (INCLUDING HANDLES)

This held ice to keep the butter pats cool. It has a loose drainer. A hand-turned butter pat machine turned out various stamped designs quite quickly.

Egg Condiment Set

3 1/8 INCHES / 8 CM HIGH

This contains an open salt cellar, dry mustard pot with hinged lid, and a removable pierced pepper pot with screw-thread lid, on three ball feet. Shown with spoon and two glass liners. Used with your boiled egg.

Salt Cellar and French Mustard Pot

3 3/4 INCHES / 9.5 CM LONG (INCLUDING HANDLE)

Shown with associated glass liners and spoons.

Grapefruit Bowl
6 INCHES / 15.25 CM DIAMETER

This silverplate grapefruit bowl
would also contain crushed ice.

Silverware used for seasoning.

Sugar Dredger
7 INCHES / 17.75 CM HIGH

This pierced caster was filled
with granulated sugar.

Powdered Sugar Dredger
6 1/2 INCHES / 16.5 CM HIGH

This has a unique plunger type
top. When turned upside down,
it dispenses a small amount of
powdered sugar. The top drops
closed again when placed upright.

Syrup Jug
6 5/8 INCHES / 16.8 CM HIGH

With hinged lid and thumb piece.

Oil and Vinegar Cruet

8 1/8 INCHES / 20.6 CM HIGH

Thomas Webb & Sons, F. & C. Osler, and Stevens & Williams all supplied cut crystal for Elkington.

Footed Salt, Pepper, Horseradish and Toothpick Holder

APPROX 3 7/5 INCHES / 9.5 CM HIGH

The lid of the horseradish pot unscrews and serves as a wand to spread the horseradish.

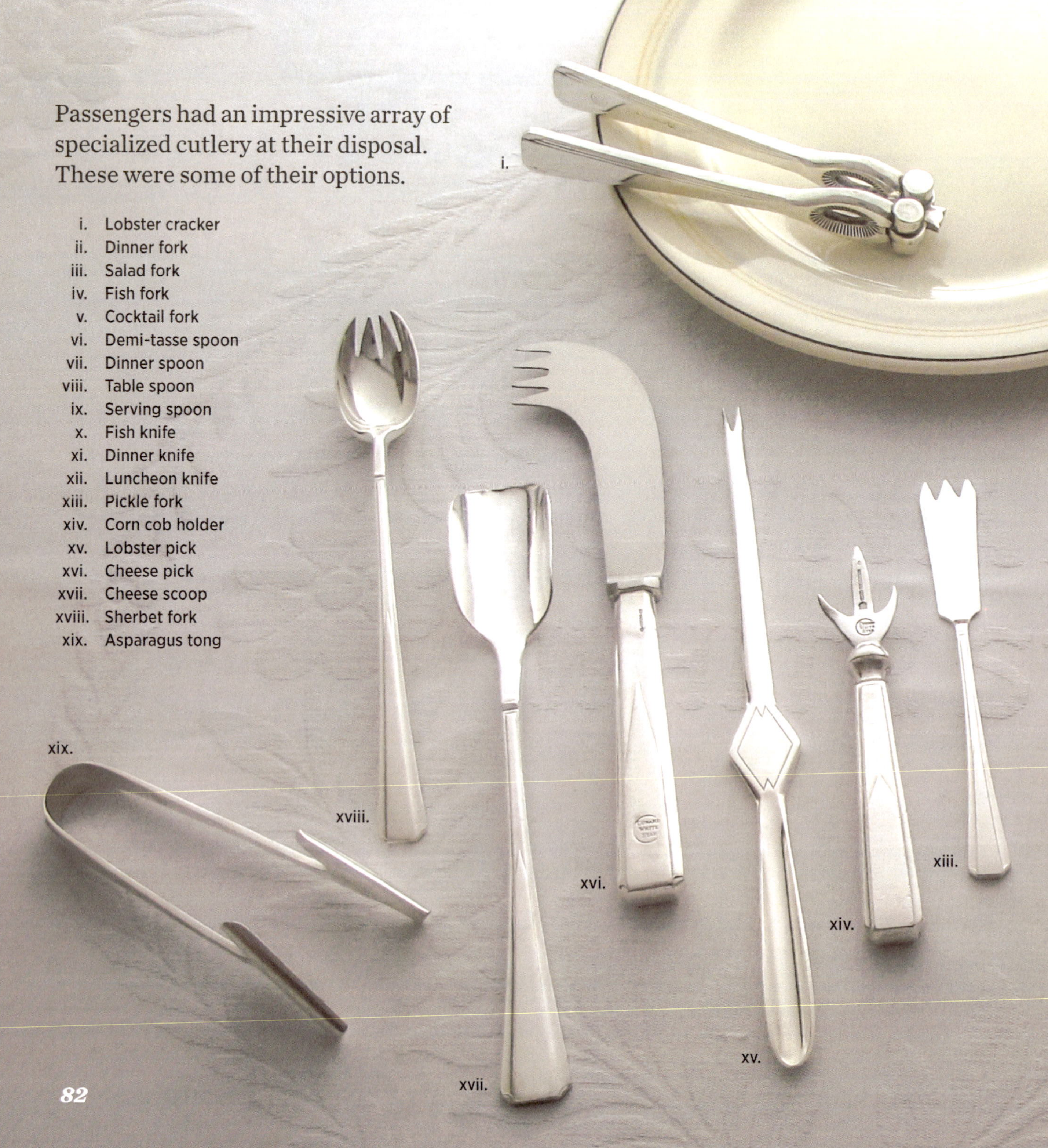

Passengers had an impressive array of specialized cutlery at their disposal. These were some of their options.

i.	Lobster cracker
ii.	Dinner fork
iii.	Salad fork
iv.	Fish fork
v.	Cocktail fork
vi.	Demi-tasse spoon
vii.	Dinner spoon
viii.	Table spoon
ix.	Serving spoon
x.	Fish knife
xi.	Dinner knife
xii.	Luncheon knife
xiii.	Pickle fork
xiv.	Corn cob holder
xv.	Lobster pick
xvi.	Cheese pick
xvii.	Cheese scoop
xviii.	Sherbet fork
xix.	Asparagus tong

82

ii.
iii.
iv.
v.
vi.
vii.
viii.
ix.
x.
xi.
xii.

Your busy Cunard White Star waiter fulfilled every culinary desire from a trolley wheeled to your tableside. Cunard White Star was renown for its quality and service.

Table Crumber

12 1/4 INCHES / 30.8 CM LONG

Also called 'Crumb Scraper' or 'Crumb Scoop.' The commis waiter would use a waiter's cloth and this pan to sweep crumbs from your cleared dining table before the dessert course.

Knife Sharpener

4 INCHES / 10 CM LONG (INCLUDING HANDLE)

Most likely found on the cart where roast beef was carved.

— COURTESY OF JONATHAN QUAYLE, PURSER'S LOCKER

Ladles

FROM 5 TO 10 INCHES / 12.7 TO 25.4 CM LONG

There is a wide variety of ladle sizes from small to large; the larger specimens were used in the ship's kitchens, while the smaller versions were used by your waiter.

At right is a passenger's seating card for breakfast, lunch and dinner. This guaranteed you your assigned table, in this case table 63 for the second sitting.

Table Number

13 3/4 INCHES/ 35 CM HIGH

The wood portion is of English Sycamore to match the first class dining room chairs. The number is an inlay using black celluloid plastic.

These signs allowed passengers to locate their assigned table easily. On the first evening of the crossing a table with a diagram of the dining room painted on the top was placed at the entrance. Passengers could reserve their seat by placing a paper with their name written on it in the corresponding slot on the table top.

Tea Strainer and Sugar Tongs

TEA STRAINER 5 INCHES / 12.7 CM LONG
SUGAR TONGS 4 1/2 INCHES / 11.4 CM LONG

Passengers relaxing on deck did not lack attention; deck stewards brought their afternoon tea on a tray. They could remain in their deck chair, wrapped snugly in a deck blanket, and sip hot tea. Although the tea pots had built in strainers, they could let in small leaves and therefore strainers were necessary. The strainers and especially the sugar tongs were coveted souvenirs, so your attentive deck steward did this for you.

Soup Tureen

7 3/4 INCHES / 19.6 CM DIAMETER
9 3/4 INCHES / 24.7 CM DIAMETER
10 1/4 INCHES / 26 CM DIAMETER
(INCLUDING HANDLES)

There are three sizes of these striking tureens in this identical shape, the design of which is at the same time ancient and truly modern. The flush handle on the cover permits economical stacking. The smallest of the tureens is just 7 3/4 inches.

— TUREEN IS THE KIND COURTESY OF TIMOTHY GARLINGHOUSE

Asparagus Server

**11 1/2 INCHES /
29.5 CM LONG**

Raised; on four feet.
There is an associated
tray and tongs.

Covers
and Round
Dishes

Some well worn
examples of covers
and trays. The round
covers were used as a plate
cover. The round
charger was used when
drinks were served
to your room.

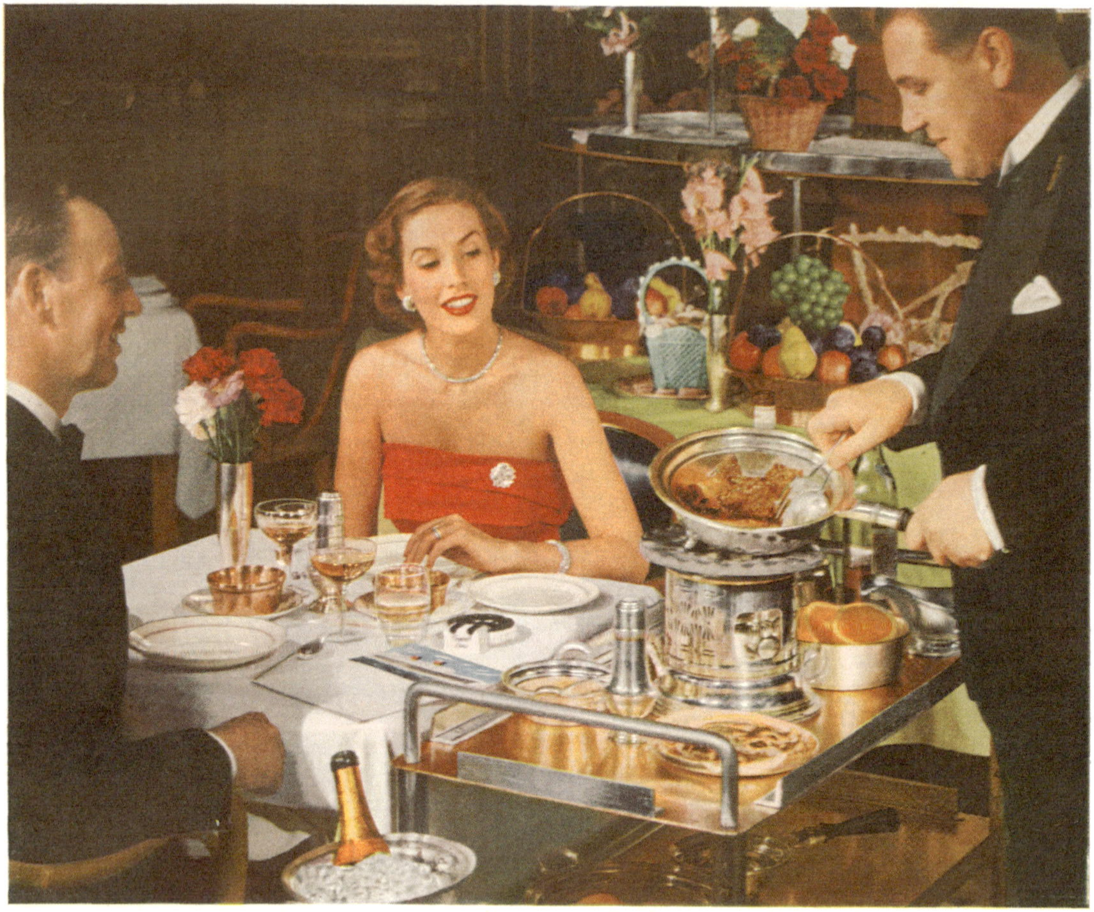

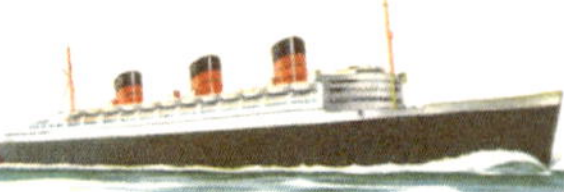

Getting there is half the *fun!*

Crepes Suzette—tempting, flavorful, liqueur-drenched . . . perfect climax to a superb meal . . . and typical of the luscious creations that make dining aboard a Cunarder a gourmet's delight! Whether you're Europe-bound or cruising to lands of romance, this is the life you'll love. Surrender yourself blissfully to days of healthful relaxation . . . breathe deeply of the clean salt air! Enjoy the charming company, the nightly fun and frivolity that make an ocean voyage via Cunard one of life's supreme pleasures! And whatever your taste in ships, there's a Cunarder to suit you —from the world's largest and fastest liners to the more leisurely.

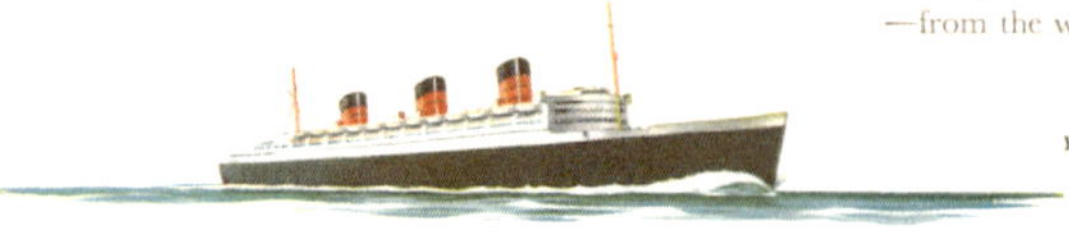

YOUR TRAVEL AGENT WILL SERVE YOU AT NO EXTRA COST

No wonder more people prefer CUNARD

QUEEN ELIZABETH · QUEEN MARY · MAURETANIA · CARONIA · BRITANNIC · MEDIA · PARTHIA

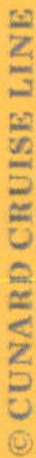

Presentation was the keynote of Cunard's famed dessert course. These items allowed headwaiters to skillfully flambé dishes like the dramatic *bombe surprise* at tableside.

Crêpe Suzette Pan

12 1/2 INCHES / 31.75 CM LONG

The *crêpe suzette* sauce would be made and set alight in this small pan.

Chafing Dish

8 1/8 INCHES / 20.6 CM HIGH

With burner and removable pan. Undoubtedly there would be a matching lid.

Table Cooking Lamp

7 5/8 INCHES / 19.25 CM HIGH

These table burners worked off an alcohol-based fuel that burned relatively cleanly. However, according to folklore it was not uncommon for the smoke from the cooking process to set off the silent smoke alarms in the first class dining room.

(Opposite page) Cunard featured 'headwaiters' preparing *crêpes suzette* tableside in many of their advertisements.

An enlargement of the
engraved cross from the base
of the chalice to the left.

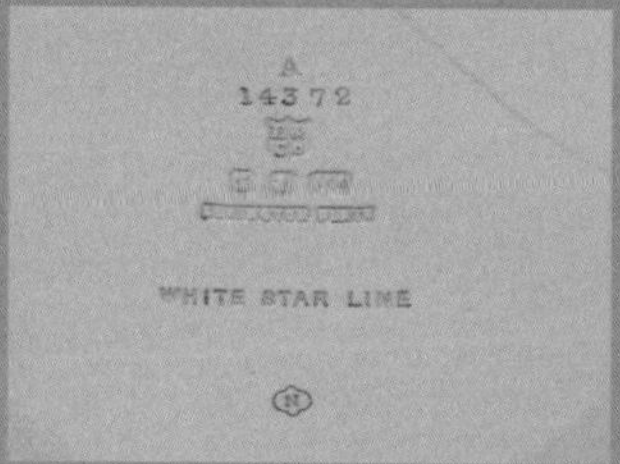

The underside of the paten
for the chalice on the right;
it is marked White Star
Line and dates to 1925.

Chalices with Patens

7 INCHES / 17.75 CM HIGH

Notice how the patens are indented to fit snugly inside the lip of the
chalice, so that the motion of a ship at sea does not dislodge it. The chalice
on the left is unmarked except for an engraved cross. On the right is a
chalice marked White Star Line; the Elkington mark dates it to 1925. Both
chalices were used on board *Queen Mary*. The frugal Cunard White Star
Line would often carry items over from ships retired in the 1930s.

— CHALICES ARE THE KIND COURTESY OF THOMAS DANIEL HOGAN IV

This 1935 Art Deco Torah Ark was located in a permanent synagogue known as the "Scroll Room" on the *Queen Mary's* third-class deck.

For those passengers who chose to worship, Cunard White Star Limited considerately offered a wide range of religious services. *Queen Mary* had a synagogue on board, along with a Catholic chapel, and of course Divine Service for those who were Church of England.

Passengers of different faiths could go to a non-denominational service on Sundays in the first class main lounge. This service was conducted by the captain.

The first class drawing room served as the first class Catholic Chapel. Second class passengers used the second class drawing room and library, and third class passengers had their own separate altar.

Orthodox Jewish passengers ordered from their own kosher menu. The *Queen Mary* was one of the first transatlantic liners to guarantee a fully kosher environment, with a separate galley stocked with a full complement of cookware, tableware and linens, along with kosher chefs and waiters. An authorized *shomer* was on board to ensure that *kasruth* or Jewish dietary laws were observed. Not only were all eating utensils marked as above, but crystal, cookware, serving utensils and even linens were marked—those by a stitched red line.

ELKINGTON MAKER'S MARKS AND DATE CODES

Elkington made the bulk of the serviceware in all classes on *Queen Mary*, but not all. Still, those exceptions were made under license to Elkington.

The earliest Elkington & Co. electroplate was stamped only with E & Co. crowned in a shield.

In 1841 a date number was added, beginning with '1'. In 1849 the series was altered to a string of letters from 'A' to 'Z' (with some exceptions), the series beginning again when the letter 'Z' was reached. The font, letter case and shield shape were changed after each year's cycle. In that manner it so happened that in 1936 the silver commissioned for hull #534 had the letter 'Z.'

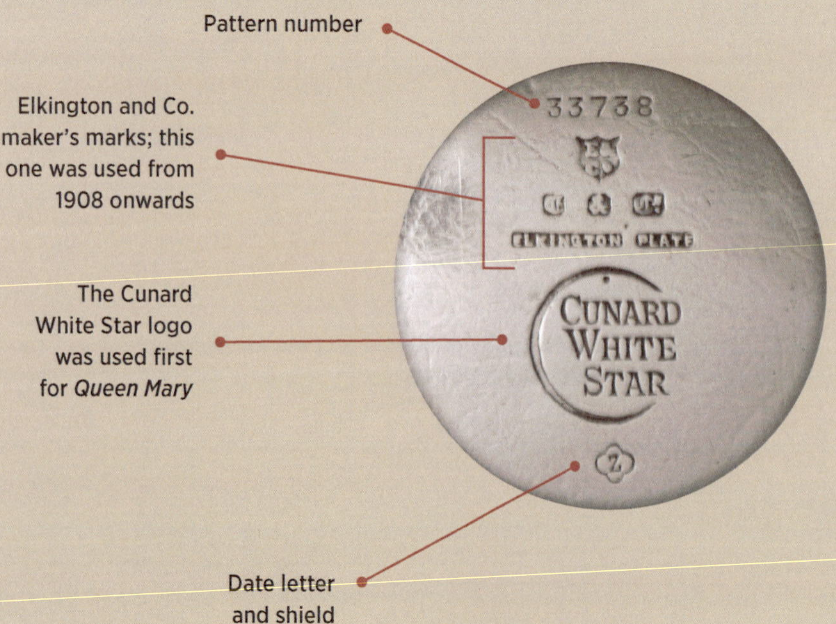

Pattern number

Elkington and Co. maker's marks; this one was used from 1908 onwards

The Cunard White Star logo was used first for *Queen Mary*

Date letter and shield

SHIELD SHAPE	LETTER/ YEAR	
		1936
	Z.	1936
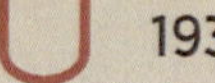		1937 thru 1960
	A.	1937
	B.	1938
	D.	1939
	E.	1940
	F.	1941
	G.	1942
	H.	1943
	I.	1944
	J.	1945
	K.	1946
	L.	1947
	M.	1948
	N.	1949
	O.	1950
	P.	1951
	R.	1952
	S.	1953
	T.	1954
	U.	1955
	V.	1956
	W.	1957
	X.	1958
	Y.	1959
	Z.	1960
		1961 thru 1967
	a.	1961
	b.	1962
	c.	1963
	d.	1964
	e.	1965
	f.	1966
	g.	1967

— DUCK PRESS AND PHOTOS ARE THE KIND COURTESY OF PAUL BIRD / TRESORS ANTIQUES

Duck Press

12 INCHES / 30.5 CM DEEP
14 INCHES / 35.5 CM WIDE
22 INCHES / 56 CM HIGH

Undoubtedly from *Aquitania*. Elkington's Acanthus leaf pattern.

Elkington manufactured the heavier weight cutlery items in the service (tea strainers, nutcrackers/seafood crackers, corn on the cob holders, salad tongs, asparagus tongs and so on), all in Plain Pine. However, the bulk of the flatware was produced under license to Roberts and Belk Ltd. The Plain Pine pattern was enjoyed by both first and second class—third class passengers made do with Embassy plate in a more traditional acanthus leaf pattern, originally designed for *Aquitania* circa 1913.

SOUVENIRS

Silver souvenir hunting caused Cunard considerable inconvenience. As early as 1922 it was estimated that souvenir hunters could cost as much as £10,000 a year in the case of a large liner. The *Cunard* magazine wrote that "despite every precaution taken to ensure the safety of silver tableware small items are surreptitiously purloined on every voyage, cream ewers, for instance, tea spoons, fish forks and pepper pots. Often, the passenger will ask for a small piece of souvenir silver to add to his collection, but more often than not the item required is simply purloined."

Offering souvenirs in the ship's shops gave passengers a guilt-free way to bring a momento of their crossing home, and assured a troublefree trip through customs.

Following pages:
A 1938 Elkington
catalog for the hotel
plate cutlery and
cooking utensils
used for RMS
Queen Mary.

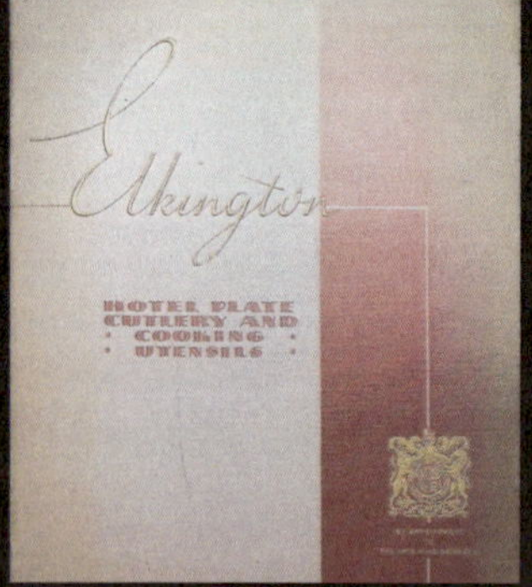

The catalog cover.

Right: An introductory page
showing 'Cabin Restaurant,
RMS *Queen Mary.*'

CABIN RESTAURANT, R.M.S. "QUEEN MARY"

Elkington Plate

USED BY THE MOST FAMOUS HOTELS, RESTAURANTS

STEAMSHIP AND RAILWAY COMPANIES

MONTREAL, TORONTO, etc.
and Agencies throughout the United
Kingdom and the World

HEAD OFFICE AND MANUFACTORY:
BIRMINGHAM, 3

Agents for Scotland & Northern Ireland:
DAVIS, DUFF & SON LTD.
25-27, ROYAL EXCHANGE SQUARE
GLASGOW
Telegrams: "Jeweller, Glasgow"
Telephone: Central 7689

ELKINGTON
& CO. LTD.

136, REGENT STREET, LONDON, W. 1
Telegrams: "Elkington, Piccy, London"   *Telephone:* Regent 1666 (5 lines)

NEWHALL STREET, BIRMINGHAM, 3
Telegrams: "Elkington, Birmingham"   *Telephone:* Central 1086

H.N.S.   V1/38

ELKINGTON & CO. LTD.

Examples of the magnificent Table Service supplied for the Cabin Restaurant of the R.M.S. "Queen Mary"

No. 35725
ELKINGTON PLATE

10 inch	...	£1	14	0
12 "	...	2	2	0
14 "	...	2	11	0
16 "	...	3	7	0
18 "	...	4	7	0
20 "	...	5	10	0
22 "	...	6	17	0
24 "	...	8	10	0

No. 31654
ELKINGTON PLATE

10 inch	...	£1	12	0
12 "	...	2	2	0
14 "	...	2	17	0
16 "	...	3	18	0

No. 37081
ELKINGTON PLATE
£3 0 0

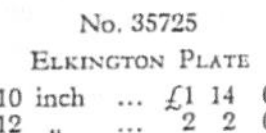

No. 35294
ELKINGTON PLATE
4 inches diameter excluding handles
£1 0 0

No. 33982
ELKINGTON PLATE
£2 10 0

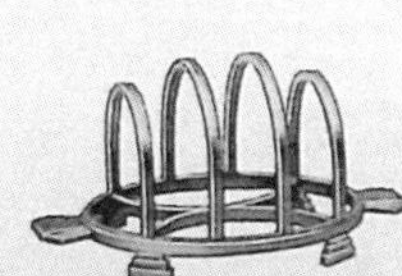

No. 33831
ELKINGTON PLATE
£1 3 0

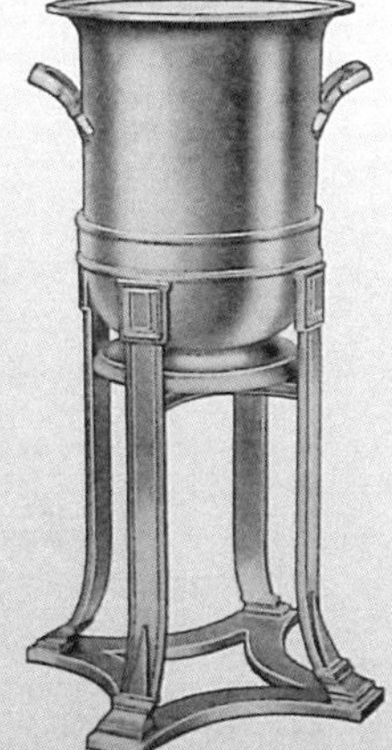

No. 32882
ELKINGTON PLATE

5 ounce capacity	...	£1	6	0
10 " "	...	2	0	0

No. 35942
ELKINGTON PLATE
6 inches diameter
£1 17 6

No. 34059
ELKINGTON PLATE
Wine Cooler, quart size £5 0 0
" " Stand 9 6 0

32

No. 36626
ELKINGTON PLATE
8½ inches diameter

Soufflé Dish	...	£2	10	0
" " lining	...	1	0	0

Left: A page titled: 'Examples of the magnificent Table Service supplied for the Cabin Restaurant of the RMS *Queen Mary*.' The items have the Elkington shape/model number. These are the numbers stamped on your silver plate.

ELKINGTON & CO. LTD.

CARVING TABLES FOR "PLAT DU JOUR" SERVICE
Two Fine Examples of Elkington Craftsmanship

Table in Solid Oak, modern in design, with extra strong ball-bearing castors. Joint Dish and Revolving Cover, Vegetable Pots, powerful Lamps, etc. Fitted with aluminium slab for carving. Length of Carving Dish, 27 inches. Width of Carving Dish, $16\frac{1}{2}$ inches. Complete as illustrated in
Elkington Plate
£140 0 0

Table in Elkington Plate throughout. In modern style, beautifully made and finished, it forms a striking piece in Grill or Dining Room.

Complete as illustrated
£176 0 0

or with the addition of a
Plate Cupboard,
£208 0 0

53

ELKINGTON & CO. LTD.

SPECIAL ITEMS FOR HIGH-CLASS CUISINE

No. 30817
Table Cooking Lamp
Specially designed with powerful lamp for heating Sauces
or Gravies on Table
Height 7½ inches.   Diameter 7 inches

ELKINGTON PLATE	...	£8 15 0
MONARCHY PLATE	...	8 11 0

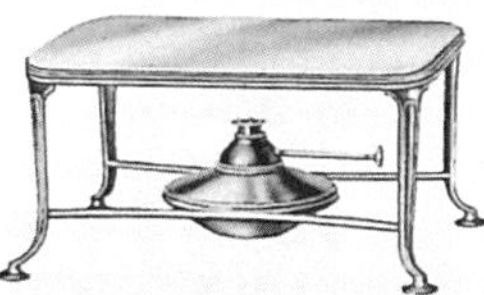

No. 30806
Aluminium Heater, for all purposes

		ELKINGTON PLATE
11 inch long, 8 inch wide, 1 Lamp	...	£4 2 0
18 „ „ 9 „ „ 2 Lamps	...	6 15 0
26 „ „ 9 „ „ 3 „	...	9 7 0

No. 30901
Duck Press
ELKINGTON PLATE ... £55 0 0
We supply these Presses in various patterns

No. 20988
Chafing Dish
With richly chased Louis XVI ornamentation

			ELKINGTON PLATE
6 inch	...	...	£8 8 0
8 „	...	...	10 15 0
10 „	...	...	14 0 0

Also made in a perfectly plain pattern

No. 20986

			ELKINGTON PLATE
6 inch	...	...	£6 0 0
8 „	...	...	7 5 0
10 „	...	...	10 10 0

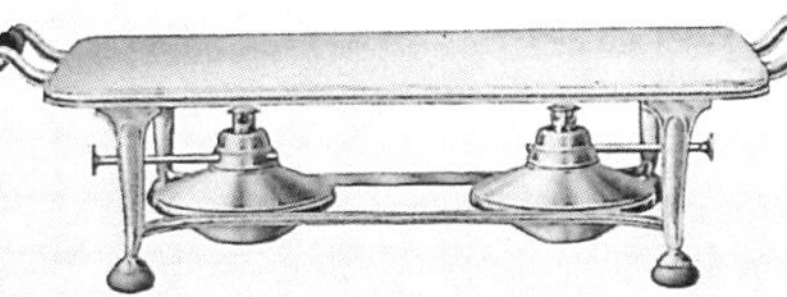

No. 849
Aluminium Heater
For all purposes
Fitted with powerful Spirit Lamps, insulated Handles and Feet,
and Aluminium Plate

		ELKINGTON PLATE
11 inch long, 8 inch wide, with 1 Lamp	...	£6 3 0
18 „ „ 9 „ „ „ 2 Lamps	...	8 15 0
26 „ „ 9 „ „ „ 3 „	...	11 6 6

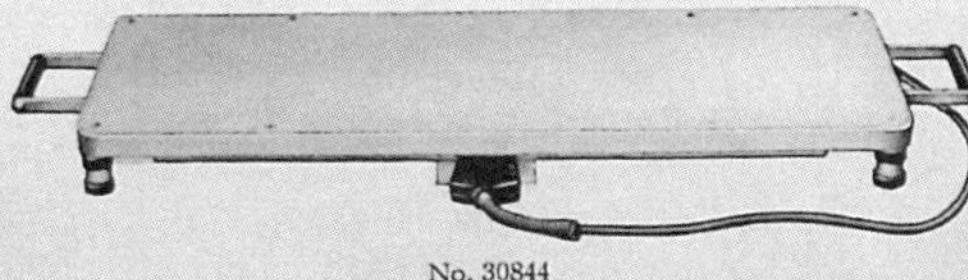

No. 30844
Fitted for Electricity

			ELKINGTON PLATE
18 inch long, 9 inch wide	...	...	... £8 10 0
24 „ „ 15 „ „	...	...	... 12 10 0
26 „ „ 9 „ „	...	...	... 10 0 0

Anderson, Anne FSA; *'The Cube Teapot: The Story of the Patent Teapot,'* 1999

Dr. Arnstein, Nelson

Dr. Feldman, Eleanor; who generously shared her notes on the Stuart Crystal
    pattern books for Cunard

Hajdamach, Charles; former Director of Broadfield House Glass Museum,
    who made it all possible

Hallett, Keith; ex-steward, RMS *Mauretania II*

Pauli, Roger; former Managing Director of Stuart Crystal, who shared his
    memories, production details and a priceless family heirloom

The Pottery Gazette and Glass Trades Review, 'The *Queen Elizabeth*,' December 1946
    courtesy *The Pottery Gazette*

Quayle, Jonathan; purserslocker.co.uk

Rushton, Ralph; ex-first and cabin class waiter, lift man, bell boy
    and bathroom steward, *Queen Mary*

The Studio: An Illustrated Magazine of Fine and Applied Art, 'The *Queen Mary*'s Silver Plate,'
    March 1936; courtesy Studio International, www.studiointernational.com

Wooders, Dave and Radford, James; '*Adventures on the* Queen Mary,' 2013

9 798234 036506